CROSLAND AND NEW L

Also by Dick Leonard

THE BACKBENCHER AND PARLIAMENT (*edited with Valentine Herman*)

THE ECONOMIST GUIDE TO THE EUROPEAN UNION

ELECTIONS IN BRITAIN TODAY

PAYING FOR PARTY POLITICS

THE SOCIALIST AGENDA: Crosland's Legacy (*edited with David Lipsey*)

WORLD ATLAS OF ELECTIONS (*with Richard Natkiel*)

Crosland and New Labour

Edited by

Dick Leonard

Postscript by Susan Crosland

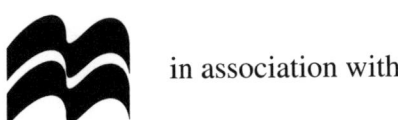 in association with

Selection, editorial matter and Chapter 1 © Dick Leonard 1999
Individual chapters (in order) © David Lipsey, Raymond Plant, Gordon Brown, Michael Young, Roy Hattersley, Christopher Price, Humphrey Cole, Michael Palliser, Brian Brivati, David Reisman, Peter Kellner, Philip Dodd, Daniel Wincott, Tony Wright, Susan Crosland 1999

All rights reserved. No reproduction, copy or transmission of this publication may be made without written permission.

No paragraph of this publication may be reproduced, copied or transmitted save with written permission or in accordance with the provisions of the Copyright, Designs and Patents Act 1988, or under the terms of any licence permitting limited copying issued by the Copyright Licensing Agency, 90 Tottenham Court Road, London W1P 9HE.

Any person who does any unauthorised act in relation to this publication may be liable to criminal prosecution and civil claims for damages.

The authors have asserted their rights to be identified as the authors of this work in accordance with the Copyright, Designs and Patents Act 1988.

First published 1999 by
MACMILLAN PRESS LTD
Houndmills, Basingstoke, Hampshire RG21 6XS
and London
Companies and representatives
throughout the world

ISBN 0–333–73989–2 hardcover
ISBN 0–333–73990–6 paperback

A catalogue record for this book is available from the British Library.

This book is printed on paper suitable for recycling and made from fully managed and sustained forest sources.

10 9 8 7 6 5 4 3 2 1
08 07 06 05 04 03 02 01 00 99

Printed and bound in Great Britain by
Antony Rowe Ltd, Chippenham, Wiltshire

Contents

Acknowledgements		vii
Notes on the Contributors		ix
1	By Way of Introduction *Dick Leonard*	1

Part I After a Generation

2	Revisionists Revise *David Lipsey*	13
3	Crosland, Equality and New Labour *Raymond Plant*	19
4	Equality – Then and Now *Gordon Brown*	35
5	Anthony Crosland and Socialism *Michael Young*	49

Part II Ministerial Record

6	Crosland as a Minister *Roy Hattersley*	57
7	Education Secretary *Christopher Price*	67
8	Environment Secretary *Humphrey Cole*	87
9	Foreign Secretary *Michael Palliser*	99

Part III Continuing Legacy

10	Crosland as Apparatchik *Brian Brivati*	107

11	Anthony Crosland as a Political Economist *David Reisman*	125
12	Equality of Access *Peter Kellner*	149
13	The Arts of Life: Crosland's Culture *Phillip Dodd*	167
14	Crosland, European Social Democracy and New Labour *Daniel Wincott*	179
15	New Labour, Old Crosland? *Tony Wright*	193
16	Postscript *Susan Crosland*	203
Index		205

Acknowledgements

Thanks are due to the Fabian Society and *The Economist*, which jointly sponsored the Crosland Memorial Meeting on 13 February 1997, which was the seedbed of this book; to *Prospect* for permission to reprint material included in Chapter 1; to Sunder Katwala of Macmillan, who first suggested the publication of the book and who has been a constant source of encouragement throughout its production; and to Paul Richards, Sir Christopher Foster and Mark Leonard for advice on its contents.

Notes on the Contributors

Brian Brivati is Reader in History at Kingston University and Director of CUSOP (Centre for Study of Society and Politics). His publications include *Hugh Gaitskell* and *New Labour in Power: Precedents and Prospects* (edited with Tim Bale). He is currently writing a history of the idea of modernisation in Labour's general election campaigns since 1945.

Gordon Brown has been Chancellor of the Exchequer since May 1997, and MP for Dunfermline East since 1983. He was Shadow Chief Secretary to the Treasury (1987–9) and Shadow Trade and Industry Secretary before becoming the Shadow Chancellor in 1992. He is the author of a number of books including *Maxton*, *The Politics of Nationalism and Devolution* and *Where There is Greed*. He has edited several books, including *John Smith: Life and Soul of the Party* and (with Tony Wright) *Values, Visions and Voices*.

Humphrey Cole was born in 1928, son of the well known Fabians, G.D.H. and Margaret Cole. After studying maths at Cambridge, and helping to found NALSO, the Labour students' organisation, he switched to economics. After work in Oxford and Paris, he joined the Government Economic Service in 1966, eventually becoming the Chief Economic Adviser to the Department of the Environment.

Susan Crosland is an author and journalist. Her memoir *Tony Crosland* was published in 1982.

Philip Dodd is Director of the Institute of Contemporary Arts and an award-winning broadcaster, writer and curator. He has written widely on culture and national identity, and relevant publications include a volume of essays on Englishness and the Demos pamphlet, *The Battle over Britain*.

Roy Hattersley is a former Deputy Leader of the Labour Party, and a member of James Callaghan's cabinet in 1976–9. He was MP for Birmingham Sparkbrook 1964–97, and is now a life peer. A prolific journalist and broadcaster, his books include *A Yorkshire Boyhood*, *Goodbye to Yorkshire*, *Politics Apart*, *Press Gang*, *Endpiece Revisited*, *Between Ourselves*, *Choose Freedom: The Future of Democratic Socialism*, *Who Goes Home?*, *Fifty Years on: A Prejudiced History of Britain since the War*, and the fiction trilogy: *The Maker's Mark*, *In That Quiet Earth*, *Skylark's Song*.

Peter Kellner is a political commentator for *The Observer*, *Evening Standard* and BBC TV *Newsnight*. A former Visiting Fellow of Nuffield College, Oxford and the Policy Studies Institute, he has contributed to or coauthored a number of books on politics, including *Fabian Essays in Socialist Thought*, *The Civil Servants: An Inquiry into Britain's Ruling Class*, *Britain's Votes 1997* and *Public Expenditure: Effective Management and Control*.

Dick Leonard was Labour MP for Romford, 1970–4, serving as Parliamentary Private Secretary to Anthony Crosland. He edited Crosland's *Socialism Now* (1974) and, with David Lipsey, *The Socialist Agenda: Crosland's Legacy* (Jonathan Cape, 1981). He was subsequently Assistant Editor of *The Economist*, and Chief Correspondent in Brussels, where he now works as Senior Adviser to the Centre for European Policy Studies. He is the author or part-author of more than a dozen books.

David Lipsey was research assistant to Anthony Crosland in 1972–4, and a special adviser to him at the

Department of the Environment and the Foreign Office, 1974–7, subsequently working for James Callaghan at 10 Downing Street. He was co-editor, with Dick Leonard, of *The Socialist Agenda: Crosland's Legacy* (Jonathan Cape, 1981). He has since held senior editorial posts on the *Sunday Times*, *New Society*, *Sunday Correspondent*, *The Times* and *The Economist*. He is a member of the Independent Commission on the Voting System and the Royal Commission on the Long-Term Care of the Elderly.

Sir Michael Palliser joined the Foreign Office in 1947. After serving in London, Athens, Paris and Dakar, he was Head of Planning Staff, a Private Secretary to the Prime Minister, Minister in Paris, British Permanent Representative to the European Communities and finally from 1975–82 (i.e. during Tony Crosland's tenure) Permanent Under-Secretary at the FCO.

Raymond Plant has been Master of St Catherine's College, Oxford since 1994, previously Professor of Politics, University of Southampton. He is a Labour Life Peer (Home Affairs spokesman, 1992–5). Author of *Hegel*, *Philosophy Politics and Citizenship*, *Political Philosophy and Social Welfare* and *Modern Political Thought*. He has published three Fabian pamphlets. He is Chair of the Fabian Commission on Taxation.

Christopher Price was Anthony Crosland's Parliamentary Private Secretary between 1966 and 1967. He has been a journalist, an MP and a university vice-chancellor; he is now Chairman of Yorkshire and Humberside Arts, a member of the Arts Council for England and edits *The Stakeholder*, a journal devoted to discussion of standards and values in public life.

David Reisman is Professor of Economics at the University of Surrey. His publications include the books

Anthony Crosland: *The Mixed Economy* (1996) and *Crosland's Future*: *Opportunity and Outcome* (1996) and related articles on "Crosland's *Future*, The First Edition", *International Journal of Social Economics*, 23 (1996); 'Crosland's *Future*: The Missing Chapter on Burnham's *Managerial Revolution*', *Research in History of Economic Thought and Methodology,* Archival Supplement 6 (1997) and 'Anthony Crosland on Equality and State', *Journal of Income Distribution*, 7 (1997).

Daniel Wincott is Lecturer in Political Science and International Studies at the University of Birmingham, having previously lectured at the University of Leicester and been Jean Monnet Lecturer in Law and Politics at the University of Warwick. He has two main areas of interest; comparative European political economy and European integration.

Tony Wright is Labour MP for Cannock Chase. Formerly Reader in Politics at Birmingham University, he is the joint editor of *Political Quarterly* and the author of many books, including *Citizens and Subjects* (1994) and *Socialisms Old and New* (1996).

Michael Young is a sociologist and entrepreneur who is founder and chairman of the School for Social Entrepreneurs which opened its doors to students in January 1997. He previously founded a string of other organisations, including the Institute of Community Studies, the Consumers' Association and the Advisory Centre for Education. His books include *The Rise of the Meritocracy,* and he is a Labour life peer.

1 By Way of Introduction*
Dick Leonard

In many ways he was an Olympian figure. Blessed with an intelligence which was several notches higher than any other politician's, with film star good looks, an incisive writing and speaking style and apparently brimming with self-confidence, it was almost written in the stars that he would rise to great heights. Added to that, his glamorous wartime record in the Parachute Regiment, his first-class honours and presidency of the Union at Oxford, his publication at the age of 38 of the widely acclaimed *The Future of Socialism*, and a glittering future seemed assured. Instead, despite some real achievements, he had a difficult and often frustrating career, and it was only in the final months of his life that it seemed that the early promise would be fulfilled.

For there was also a downside. His prodigious gifts provoked as much envy and resentment as admiration. His complex character embraced a large dose of diffidence and moral fastidiousness, which frequently led to accusations of indecisiveness. His cutting wit threatened as much as it amused, and his warm heartedness and concern and loyalty for his friends did not communicate itself to the wider public, to whom he too often conveyed an hauteur which was alien to his real nature.

He was also the victim of ill luck. Hugh Gaitskell's sudden death in 1963 almost certainly cost him the chance of becoming Chancellor of the Exchequer

---

* Revised and expanded version of an article originally published in *Prospect*.

when a Labour government was formed the following year. He again narrowly missed the chancellorship after the devaluation of 1967, when James Callaghan resigned and recommended him as his successor. Instead, Harold Wilson chose Roy Jenkins, probably because that was the simplest way of keeping Callaghan in the government, by doing a straight swap between the Treasury and the Home Office. This also had the unfortunate effect of souring future relations between the two men who had been close friends since their Oxford days, and whose views and outlook were more similar than either of them would subsequently admit.

The consequence was that throughout Wilson's long tenure as Labour leader and Prime Minister Crosland's talents were under-utilised. He held five ministerial posts, including important cabinet portfolios, but he was kept out of the top jobs. It was only when Callaghan became Prime Minister in March 1976 that he was promoted to Foreign Secretary, a post he had never sought and initially regarded as no better than a consolation prize. Callaghan hinted that he would soon swap jobs with the Chancellor, Denis Healey, and I was surprised when Crosland confided to me over lunch, eight days before his death, that he no longer expected this exchange to take place, and indeed that he rather hoped that it would not, as he found himself responding with growing enthusiasm to the challenges of the Foreign Office.

Whatever his own expectations, it was undoubtedly true that most people thought he would shortly move to the Treasury, and for the first time he was being seriously regarded as a likely successor to Callaghan as Labour leader and Prime Minister. It was not to be – he was struck down by a severe stroke on 12 February 1977, and died six days later at 58, a similar age to his close friend and mentor, Hugh Gaitskell.

With Labour again in power, now is a good time not only to reassess Crosland's career, but also the relevance of his writings to the problems which confront the Blair government. This task has been greatly simplified by two books recently published by David Reisman, a contributor to the present volume – *Anthony Crosland: The Mixed Economy* and *Crosland's Future: Opportunity and Outcome* (both Macmillan, 1996).

Reisman has been nothing if not thorough. He seems to have traced every word that Crosland ever published – his four books, *Britain's Economic Problem* (1953), *The Future of Socialism* (1956), *The Conservative Enemy* (1962) and *Socialism Now* (1974), a quiverful of Fabian pamphlets and a large number of articles in newspapers, magazines and academic journals. He also made imaginative use of the Crosland archive at the LSE library, which contains his undergraduate essays and the remarkable correspondence which Crosland maintained, throughout the war years, with his boyhood and university friend Philip Williams, later a distinguished political scientist at Nuffield College and the biographer of Gaitskell. In these letters Crosland's intellectual and political development can be traced step by step as he discusses contemporary issues with Williams, and reflects on the books he was reading.

He was consequently able to provide a comprehensive account of Crosland's views on every subject he discussed, tracing their origin and development over time, revealing in the process a high degree of consistency. He also took full account of Crosland's critics, and – generally very fairly – discussed the extent to which he was able, as a minister, to give practical effect to the policies which he had advocated.

Reisman had little difficulty in tracing Crosland's intellectual antecedents. Apart from the German revisionist Marxist, Eduard Bernstein, he named three economists – Alfred Marshall, A.C. Pigou and Hugh Dalton – as seminal influences, as well as five more political writers who had speculated on the future of democratic socialism in the interwar period of depression and poverty. These were G.D.H. Cole, R.H. Tawney, Evan Durbin, Douglas Jay and again – in a different guise – Hugh Dalton.

Yet the Socialism which Crosland preached was not something dreamed up out of books. He looked round the democratic world and identified two role-models. The first of these was the USA. He was immensely attracted by its openness, its dynamism and the absence of class barriers. As Reisman put it, 'Crosland had seen the future and had seen that it works...he had found a convergent and classless culture in which ordinary people had spontaneously built equality into their way of life.' In Crosland's own words in *The Future of Socialism*:

> One of the strong attractions of American society is the extraordinary social freedom, the relaxed, informal atmosphere, the easier contacts, the relative natural assumption of equality, the total absence of deference and the relative absence of snobbery and of that faint, intangible but none the less insistent sense of class that penetrates social attitudes in Britain.

Crosland's youthful love affair with the USA, which did not noticeably diminish with the years, was unusual for a Socialist, and even his close friend Michael Young tried to persuade him to tone down his enthusiasm in a letter commenting on an early draft of the book. Crosland, who normally showed great respect for Young's views, ignored his advice.

His other great role-model was, of course, Sweden, where he greatly admired the progress made in eliminating poverty and achieving a wide measure of social and economic equality. This, he observed, owed nothing to nationalisation proposals, but was due to intelligent use of the government's general economic powers and, in particular, by pushing redistributive taxation further than in any other democracy. It was no accident that one of the chapter headings in *The Future of Socialism* (to which the Left took especial exception) was 'The Growing Irrelevance of the Ownership of the Means of Production'.

If anybody doubts the impact which Sweden and the USA had on the young Crosland, they have only to consult the index of *The Future of Socialism*. The USA figures 42 times, and Sweden (sometimes bracketed with other Scandinavian countries) 38. There are 10 references each to the Soviet Union (mostly negative) and Germany. But no other country merits more than *two* mentions.

What was it that the USA and Sweden had in common which distinguished them so sharply from the Great Britain of 1956 (and still at the start of the new millennium)? It was, Crosland was quick to notice, that in neither country was there an extensive and prestigious system of private schooling. With few exceptions, the American High School and the Swedish *folkskola* were attended alike by the sons and daughters of bosses and of workers, who grew up with a common culture and little feeling of social distance. He identified the 'public' schools (one of which – Highgate – he had himself attended) as the key element in the persistence of social stratification in Britain.

Reisman criticised Crosland's role as Education Secretary in 1965–7 when, he asserted, he was considerably less radical than his writings would have led one to expect. By not using compulsion, he alleges, the movement towards comprehensive schools was slower than it need have been. Yet Crosland – who always preferred persuasion to cracking the whip – succeeded in jollying along local education authorities so successfully that 83 per cent of secondary school pupils were being educated comprehensively by the end of the Labour government.

On 'public' schools his criticism may be more valid. Crosland lacked the resources to integrate them into the public system, and his libertarian principles excluded making it an offence to pay for private schooling. Yet he made no attempt to pursue the course advocated by his friend John Vaizey, who correctly identified that the main practical appeal to wealthy parents of the public schools was that they enabled them to buy privileged access to the ancient (state-funded) universities. The private sector of education, Vaizey wrote, amounted to 5 per cent of the whole: if their pupils were restricted to 5 per cent of the places at Oxford and Cambridge their appeal to rational parents would rapidly diminish.

Crosland was aware of Vaizey's proposal, but he did not try to implement it. Instead, he set up a toothless Public Schools' Commission, which eventually produced proposals similar to the Tories' later assisted places' scheme. Michael Young and Christopher Price, in Chapters 5 and 7 in the present volume, concur in the view that Crosland, who was fanatical in his prioritisation, did not act because he thought that comprehensivisation and the expansion of higher education were more pressing objectives.

Nearly a generation after Crosland's death, many of his prescriptions have become unfashionable, even on the democratic left. The tax-and-spend policies, with which he was most associated (though he did say, in a famous phrase in 1975, 'the party's over') have been disowned by New Labour. Sweden and the USA have lost much of their shine, and enthusiasm for the comprehensive schools has waned. He himself never thought that *The Future of Socialism* was written in stone, and acknowledged some second thoughts, the main one being that he had grossly under-estimated the difficulty of achieving sufficient growth to pay for the relatively painless progression to the good society that he sought. Nor did he anticipate the apparently intractable problem of structural unemployment which has afflicted most of western Europe since the 1970s, nor the strong appeal of Tory tax-cutting populism.

So, 40 or so years after it was written, his master work will hardly do as a blueprint for New Labour. Yet it remains the most persuasive, eloquent and comprehensive presentation of the values of democratic socialism so far attempted, and is likely to entrance and infuriate new readers for many years to come.

Would Crosland, if he were alive today, be an enthusiastic supporter of Tony Blair and New Labour? One cannot be sure, but I believe that he would, though he might find some aspects of New Labour's programme difficult to swallow. I think, in particular, of the pledge not to raise levels of income tax during the present Parliament. He was on record as not being in favour of increasing income tax rates, which he believed were already close to the level where their disincentive effects would outweigh their revenue-raising and redistributive benefits. Yet the standard rate when he died was 35 per cent, and the maximum rate on earned income was 83 per cent. It is questionable whether he would have regarded levels of 23 and 40 per cent in the same light

The main purpose of the present volume is to probe what lessons may be drawn for New Labour from Crosland's writings and from his political and ministerial career. It stems from a Memorial meeting held in London on 13 February 1997 to mark the 20th anniversary of his death. Sponsored by *The Economist*, and organised by the Fabian Society, it was attended by a large audience, which included former Prime Minister James Callaghan and other cabinet colleagues, as well as people who were closely associated with virtually every facet of Tony Crosland's life.

The main speeches were made by David Lipsey, Raymond Plant and Gordon Brown, and other contributions were made from the floor, including by Michael Young, perhaps his oldest surviving friend, and by Christopher Price, his former Parliamentary Private Secretary.

It was subsequently felt that a more permanent record should be made of the occasion, and the speakers readily agreed to revise and update their contributions in the light of the first year's experience of the Labour government which was elected shortly after the meeting. A dozen additional essays were also commissioned. The book, as it has emerged, is divided into three sections. Part I (Chapters 2–5) consists of revised and expanded versions of the platform speeches from the Memorial meeting, together with a tribute by Michael Young.

In Part II, (Chapters 6–9) Crosland's overall record as minister is assessed by Roy Hattersley, while Christopher Price, Humphrey Cole and Michael Palliser discuss his performance respectively as Education, Environment and Foreign Secretary. All four writers were closely associated with Crosland during his periods as a minister

In Part III (Chapters 10–14), various mostly younger authors, not all of whom were personally acquainted with Crosland, consider his contribution in a number of different fields, and Tony Wright attempts a summing up. Susan Crosland concludes the volume with a personal postscript.

Each author draws on his own knowledge and experience to describe the rich impact which Crosland made, both through his writings and his work, on a exceptionally wide range of policy areas still of relevance today. Their individual assessments and conclusions differ, but all would probably agree on two outstanding characteristics which distinguished Crosland as a political thinker and actor. One was the exceptional importance which he – like R.H. Tawney before him – attached to the principle of equality, while recognising the complexity of translating it into practical policies. The second was the sharp distinction which he drew – perhaps more cogently than any other writer – between means and ends, between policies and underlying values. The ultimate success of New Labour and the Blair government may well depend, to a large extent, on the strength of their commitment to these principles and their skill in translating them into effective action.

Part I
After a Generation

2 Revisionists Revise*
David Lipsey

1997 marked the 20th anniversary of Tony Crosland's death. There are many still active in Labour politics today who knew him, and remember him today as if 20 years was 20 days, but this is not the place for personal tributes. This volume is about the thought, not the man; about the legacy of his revisionist social democracy 20 years on, and 40 years after his greatest work, *The Future of Socialism*.

Even today, I am often approached by people who want to ask me (or tell me) what Crosland would have thought about some contemporary problem in socialist thought. What would he have thought about Europe? About proportional representation and constitutional reform generally? About (most insistent question of all) about equality?

There is only one of these questions to which I give a confident reply. Despite the fond hopes of some, we may be sure Tony would not have joined the Social Democratic Party in the early 1980s. Indeed he would be delighted that so many of its members rejoined the Labour Party in the 1990s, and thrilled by its election victory in May 1997.

Beyond that, I am not at all sure that this searching after the views of dead heroes is a valuable exercise. First, it is guesswork – inspired guesswork, maybe – but always guesswork. Secondly, the pace of history being what it is, it is not really clear how much it has to offer us. Because in the circumstances of the 1960s and 1970s Crosland was a Keynesian, it doesn't at all follow that he would be a Keynesian today.

---

* Revised and expanded version of platform speech, Memorial meeting (13 February 1997).

Thirdly, the search for these answers contains an intellectual confusion. The question asks what Crosland would have thought. But like any politician, Crosland was not a creature of pure intellect. His thought sprang from his particular historical experiences. To take an example, a man of his generation, who had served in war, was likely to have a particular view of Europe, a disposition in its favour as a guarantor of peace. He described himself as a 'sceptical pro', though as his life went on the 'sceptical' was more evident and the 'pro' less. Anyway, the historical arguments for Europe clearly have less force for a modern post-Cold War generation. The interesting question is not what Crosland would think. It is this: what would a politician of his intellect and temperament but who reached the peak of his powers today think? And the two may be by no means the same thing.

There is however one thing which Crosland would certainly have remained. He would have remained a revisionist. Let us be clear what that means. 'Revisionism' was not and is not a body of doctrine. It was not what Crosland's beloved Bernstein thought. Revisionism was and is a cast of mind. It is a cast of mind that says: here is the world, here are the most important facts about it, here are the values we bring to bear on the facts, here are our conclusions. Indeed he was always looking to see who would be writing the new *Future of Socialism* for a changing world.

I sometimes hear accusations against the present party leadership that they have abandoned the principles of revisionism. I hear them not only from the old Labour left, but from some of the old Labour democratic socialists too. And I think they miss the point.

Revisionists revise. Since Crosland, there have been some obvious and important changes in the world. Globalisation. The decline of class in general and numerically of the working class in particular. Higher unemployment levels. A taxpayers' revolt. Now we can argue and should argue about how far these changes have taken us, and what precisely are their implications for democratic socialism. Personally, for what it is worth, I think that the Labour leadership has gone further than was absolutely necessary away from the party's traditional commitment to the collective provision of public services, and its contribution to practical equality.

But revisionists revise. Given the pressures on the modern politician, I think it is remarkable how much rethinking has gone on about the fundamentals by New Labour. We may not always agree with its conclusions. But the activity of rethinking is absolutely revisionist, absolutely Croslandite.

'Always facing it, Captain McWhirr, that's the way to get through', said Joseph Conrad in a favourite Crosland quotation from *Typhoon*, once memorably used by Michael Foot in 1975 to quell a recalcitrant Labour party conference, and that is something that Croslandite revisionism leaves us with today.

I want to draw attention to a second legacy. It is this: that no one in the party drew with the same clarity before him a distinction that was central to Crosland's thought: that between means and ends. That, at base, was what motivated him in his arguments against the fundamentalist believers in public ownership. He was not particularly against public ownership *per se*; indeed, arguably as a minister he did a bit too much of it, seeking to municipalise rented property and take over development land. But his point was this: that there was nothing intrinsically superior about public ownership over private ownership. It all depended which did most to advance democratic socialist objectives: both the objectives democratic socialists shared with other political parties (such as national prosperity) and the objectives which were their own (such as greater equality).

Tony Blair, of course, drew on this distinction between ends and means heavily in his successful campaign to rewrite Clause Four of the party constitution. But it has yet to do all its work for the party.

To take one example: education. Now it is well known that Tony held strong views on comprehensive education. He was devoted to (I won't use his exact words in mixed company) getting rid of grammar schools. But this was a means to an end: more equal opportunities. So it doesn't for example follow that he would have become a supporter of some of the once-trendy more extreme interpretations of the comprehensive principle. For example it does not follow that he would have been against streaming in comprehensive schools, which is in fact essential if they are to offer the opportunities for self-betterment which equality of opportunity implies. If the policies are wrong to achieve the aims, get rid of them. That is revisionism.

To take another example, there is still a confusion between ends and means in the party in the field of public services. The end, decent public services, is still more or less consensual in the party. What is not consensual yet is the means to achieve that end.

I think for instance of market reforms of the National Health Service and of GP fundholding. There is a right debate to be held about these, which is about whether they do or do not promote a better, more cost-effective and fair service to patients. Unfortunately, it is all too easy for Labour people to fall into a wrong debate about these things – that is, a debate that assumes that any way of running these services other than through direct state provision is in some way contrary to the principles of democratic socialism. It isn't. The services are the end. The means are those that best deliver them.

A third example is welfare. The end – the alleviation of poverty – is and must remain a priority goal for all socialists. However, that does not imply that the means must remain the same – in particular that they should centre on large increases in welfare spending. Over the past 50 years, the security bill has risen eightfold in real terms. But few would suggest that there has been a commensurate improvement in the living standards of welfare recipients.

There are no simple answers. Welfare-to-work is clearly right in principle, though nobody should delude themselves that it will be a money-saver in the short run. Fraud-busting is not a right-wing policy when many people are abusing the system to extract money from the pockets of hard-working people via the taxpayer for their own benefit. But equally, the end must not be lost sight of in debating the means. There is an omnipresent danger of stigmatising the poor and thus eventually undermining the social consensus for their support.

Ends and means; means and ends: keep them separate and you will be further along the road to getting the right means to serve your ends, the policies to deliver the values. This at root was Crosland's creed; and if we take to heart no other lesson from his legacy a firm grasp of the ends and means distinction will save us from much error.

3 Crosland, Equality and New Labour*
Raymond Plant

Crosland was both a democratic socialist and a revisionist. His democratic socialism had as its aim a more socially just society, by which he meant a society which would have achieved a greater level of social and economic equality to go alongside equality in civil and political rights. He was a revisionist in that he believed that what policies were required to achieve greater social justice and equality depended upon an understanding of the major social and economic factors at work within the national economy and in the wider world at a particular time in the pattern of economic development of a specific country. Although for Crosland the ends of democratic socialism were universal, there were no necessary or intrinsic means to the achievement of these ends. They would depend crucially upon circumstance. The link between values and revisionism is however very important because it was the commitment to the goals, purposes and values of socialism, understood for Crosland in terms of social justice and greater equality, that prevented politics becoming just a rather fragmented set of problem-solving techniques. The techniques of politics and economic management had to be linked to an overarching set of values and it is in this context that his account of revisionism has to be set. Given that times change, there is no eternal or universal content to revisionism: that would be an oxymoron. What needed to be revised would change

---

* Revised and expanded version of platform speech, Memorial meeting (13 February 1997).

from time to time, but for a revisionist socialist, as I have said, this approach was to be guided in a fundamental way by values.

For Crosland himself revisionism in the 1950s was directed towards Marxist inspired forms of socialism and in particular to the view that greater social justice could be attained only by the public ownership of the basic means of production in society. The impact of Marxism was an obvious revisionist concern. After all, the Soviet Union had been created ostensibly as a Marxist state, eastern Europe had been forced into this ambit by the end of the war and Marx's work provided a template for the understanding of modern society which many found to be an inspirational guide in left-wing parties in Western Europe. However, Marx's socialism was antithetical to Crosland's own conception of it which was more social democratic in conception. In *The Critique of the Gotha Programme,* which Marx wrote as a fundamental critique of German social democracy, he argued that social democracy and democratic socialism dealt only with the symptoms of injustice in society, leaving untouched injustice in the distribution of the ownership of the means of production. For Marx, the injustice in the distribution of opportunity, in goods and services, benefits and burdens in society reflected injustice in the ownership of the means of production and could be rectified only by the common ownership of the means of production. This in turn was not going to be achieved by democratic means so far as Marx could see, and would depend on revolution.

Crosland rejected this view, which questioned the very central premises of his own morally-based conception of democratic socialism, which was fundamentally concerned with rectifying distributive injustices and which could coexist with a mixed economy and large-scale private ownership of the means of production. It was therefore central as we shall see to Crosland's revisionism that issues of production and distribution could be separated in ways that Marx would have regarded as impossible. For Crosland, the common ownership, or nationalisation of the means of production was not a necessary or intrinsic means to the achievement of socialism as it was for Marx. The question of nationalisation had to be considered in a wholly empirical rather than ideological way: that is to say would nationalisation of an industrial sector contribute towards the achievement of greater social justice and equality?. One could not take the *a priori* view and argue that it was a pervasive necessary means to the achievement of these ends. While Crosland believed that Marx deserved praise for his insights into some aspects of the nature of mid nineteenth century capitalism and its associated forms of politics, Crosland believed that Marx was a very poor guide to postwar British and Western European capitalism, which he believed had been fundamentally transformed by a whole number of interlocking factors. This is not the place for a detailed exposition of Crosland's arguments or for an evaluation of them, but he believed five things in respect of the modern Western European economies.

(1) Ownership had become dispersed amongst wider and wider groups of shareholders and therefore that management and its social responsibilities was now more important than ownership. Shareholding and its dispersal now meant that 'owners' were less able to exert power and control over what they had a fragmented share in owning. The policies and priorities of enterprises were now determined much more by managers. On the one hand Crosland saw this 'managerial revolution', as James Burnham had called it, as important as posing a fundamental problem for Marx's understanding of the nature of modern economies. At the same time he saw the emergence of the socio-economic role of the manager

as throwing up a new set of issues: To whom was the manager properly accountable? Which interests should the management of a firm properly take into account? How could the social responsibility of management be secured? These points were also made by Keynes in a not dissimilar way some years before, but it was Crosland who wove them into a critique of Marx. The growing divorce between ownership and control had led to the need for a revision of Marxist theories about this link, but nevertheless the change had led to new problems which would be very important to solve as part of the attempt to produce a revised form of social democracy.

(2) Keynesian economic management meant that government was able to manage the macro economic environment within which firms operate, which meant that politics in this sense was much more important than Marx had believed and that the ability to manipulate this wider environment meant that firms had to be more responsive to government priorities. It was again central to Marx's account of the centrality of the economic basis of society, comprising as it did for Marx the means of production (that is to say: labour, tools and raw materials) and the relations of production, (that is to say: the class relations linked to specific historical forms of production), that politics was relatively inert in producing socio–economic change. In the same way as for Marx the pattern of ownership of the means of production would shape in a fundamental and politically unalterable manner the ways in which goods and services were distributed in the economy, so class relations and economic drivers provided the fundamental political interests in society which could not be reshaped or bent to other purposes by politicians and bureaucracies. Fundamental social change would emerge from changes in the means of production, producing corresponding changes in the class structure. This process could not

be procured by politics, although once it was underway, politics could make some impact on it.

Crosland believed, however, that the growth of new economic techniques, particularly those in Keynes' *General Theory* meant that politics and government could play far more of an initiating and managing role than Marx had assumed. The development of these techniques secured a degree of autonomy of politics from economics, and allowed politicians the sense that it was possible to manage an economy and, to social democrat or democratic socialist politicians, that this could be done to achieve the values of social justice and greater equality.

(3) He believed that unions were a countervailing power to capital. On the Marxian view the owners of the means of production, the capitalist class, possessed the ultimate power in a capitalist society. This power could not ultimately be constrained either within the state or within civil society. Crosland took the view that this had just been proved historically not to be the case and that since the Second World War, the trades unions had secured a position in the organisation of industry that constrained the power of the owners of the means of production (who were, as we have already seen, in Crosland's view dispersed and could not act in a cohesive way).

(4) Similarly he thought that democratisation and the weight of politics could constrain economic imperatives, which were not like laws of nature but could be manipulated by politics.

(5) He also argued that the welfare state had made it possible to give working people a degree of security which could be achieved outside of the market. This in turn acted as a kind of constraint on the market because working people were not, in relation to wage contracts, at the mercy of employers in circumstances in which the employee had nothing to sell other than his labour power which was his only property. That

might have been true of some elements of the working class in the mid nineteenth century, but was no longer true when there is social protection and social security available. So again developments in modern society had made Marx's own account of capitalism redundant.

For these and other reasons Crosland rejected the Marxist analysis at least in so far as it applied to postwar economies and maintained that social justice could be achieved by political means and in particular without further nationalisation of the means of production. So if social democracy–democratic socialism is, *pace* Marx, a viable project in the modern world, seeking the achievement of social justice and equality, how did Crosland think about these values?

Perhaps the easiest way into answering these questions is to point out that for him social justice meant primarily an aspiration towards greater social equality, but he held a complex view of equality which meant a rejection both of equality of opportunity and equality of outcome. As an alternative he allied his view to what Rawls was later to call 'democratic equality', a view which he endorsed in *Socialism Now*.

Equality of outcome was inefficient in that unequal rewards are necessary to mobilise talent in a free society which does not direct labour (about which more below). It is also potentially a threat to liberty in that the state would have to take a very substantial degree of control over economic life if it was to ensure that the desirable level of equality of outcome was to be sustained. This degree of state control is incompatible with a mixed economy and political pluralism So he was in favour of a degree of inequality – or, to put the point another way, he thought that there were justified inequalities, but the nature of the justification is complex and will be discussed later.

He equally rejected an unqualified view of equality of opportunity.

First of all he believed that equality of opportunity against a background of pre-existing inequality would give the greatest rewards to those with fortunate family backgrounds and genetic endowment. There had to be investment, particularly in education, which would compensate for this and to try, as far as it was within the power of politics, to render starting points fairer. This is particularly so when we reflect on the fact that we do not deserve our genetic endowment or fortunate background, so we cannot use the claim that those better endowed deserve the extra rewards they may be able to secure in the economy, a point which Rawls in *A Theory of Justice* went on to elaborate in a very telling way. Crosland however, makes the point in *The Future of Socialism* wholly unambiguously:

> No one deserves either so generous a reward or so severe a penalty for a quality implanted from the outside and for which he can claim only a limited responsibility.

The point was reiterated in *Socialism Now* after he had read Rawls:

> By equality, we meant more than a meritocratic society of equal opportunities in which the greatest rewards would go to those with the most fortunate genetic endowment and family background.

So he firmly rejects the idea of meritocracy if it is imposed upon the existing structure of inequality, including not just the existing reward structure, but also the inequalities of endowment and environment. Strenuous efforts would have to be made through social and public policy, in so far as these things could be reached by collective action, to compensate and improve these initial starting points.

He also took the now rather unfashionable view that a meritocratic society which produced rewards for only marketable skills neglected a whole range of other human qualities which were vitally important for sustaining a civilised democratic society. We need to positively value a wider range of skills and human virtues than those which were realised in the economy and the labour market. There are perhaps some echoes here of some of the critical view of capitalism developed by Keynes and T.S. Eliot – that if our understanding of human worth and dignity is reduced to what is valued in the market or what mobilises people in the market, then capitalism may offer a very unsatisfactory picture of human society and human fulfilment which could become an acute problem if economic growth and wellbeing were to falter and we have no other moral resources on which to fall back.

So we can see that there is a clear rejection of both equality of outcome and an unqualified approach to equality of opportunity. In its place, as I have said he put a more complex idea which, following his use of the term in *Socialism Now,* we might as well follow Rawls into calling 'democratic equality'. By democratic equality he meant that there was clearly a case for economic inequality in the interests of efficiency and economic growth but that:

(1) These inequalities should be to the benefit of all, including the worst off. Those who attained differentially high positions should be judged not by their personal deserts because these reflected prior family and indeed genetic endowments for which individuals could not claim full responsibility; rather, economic inequalities were to be judged by the rent of ability – that is to say, what had to be paid to ensure that scarce talents the exercise of which would be in the interests of all were mobilised.

(2) That these differentially rewarded positions should be open to fair equality of opportunity – that is to say, with compensation particularly through education for poor starting points. This was a fundamental

duty on government which could legitimately spend public money on collective provision which would have a differentially helpful effect on the worst off including those with more limited genetic endowment and with poor family backgrounds.

(3) Democratic equality would not therefore leave the reward structure untouched. It was not a case of creating equality of opportunity to compete fairly against the existing pattern of rewards but also that the tax system and so forth had to be sensitive to the rent of ability which would put a constraint on this structure.

We now need to turn to an examination of the strategy to be adopted to secure this understanding of equality and social justice. There were two interlinked features of this strategy. First of all, he argued that greater equality could be gained most easily by economic growth. This would enable two things to happen:

(a) It would be a levelling-up strategy, not a levelling-down one. He was acutely aware that it would be difficult, if not impossible, in a democratic society for a majority to vote for greater equality if that was a threat to their own standard of living. By 'greater equality' here I mean the tax which would have to be levied if collective action to improve the equality of starting points was to be undertaken. This tax would be less necessary and people would be less reluctant to pay it in circumstances of high economic growth.

(b) The fiscal dividends of growth would therefore allow the better off to retain broadly speaking their absolute standard of living while improving the relative standards of the worst off.

(4) In addition, educational investment and reform in a comprehensive direction was vital if unfortunate family background and genetic endowment was to be compensated for.

Despite surface similarities his conception of democratic equality was quite different from a New Right or economic liberal perspective. The economic liberal is not interested in relative positions or the gap between rich and poor which was vital for Crosland. For the New Right what matters to the poor is whether they are better off this year than last – i.e. their absolute position not their position relative to the better off. The New Right strategy is in fact exactly the opposite of Crosland's. They believe that the trickle-down effect of the economic market will improve the absolute position of the worst off while improving the relative position of the better off. For Crosland as a democratic egalitarian, economic growth and its fiscal dividends would improve the relative position of the worst off while maintaining the standard of living of the better off.

The Labour government elected in May 1997 is self-consciously revisionist, so what are the continuities and discontinuities?

Of course, one would not expect continuities in terms of means, since the whole point of revisionism is that means have to be changed in the light of changed circumstances. So what about ends ?

It is sometimes argued that New Labour has lost interest in the idea of equality, or at least in any Croslandite understanding of equality. I think that this is probably a mistake. As I have argued, Crosland had a nuanced view of equality and did not believe in some form of strict equality of outcome. Rather he believed, as I have said, in democratic equality, or an account of legitimate inequalities, the degree of inequality being linked to and justified by the rent of ability and economic efficiency. So democratic equality certainly implies a degree of inequality, but also that such inequalities stand in need of justification and that they are not to be justified in terms of the claims of the merits of those who benefit from the degree of inequality but rather in terms of rent of ability or contribution to the economic health of society, including the relative position of the worst off which should certainly be improved. The important thing against this background conception of equality was to ensure the fairest degree of equality of opportunity to achieve what one could within a society marked by such a conception of equality. There is no doubt that New Labour is committed to equality of opportunity as an ideal and this indeed underpins their approach to employability skills and education; what is not so clear is the extent to which the government is interested in the relative as opposed to the absolute position of the poor. This is a very important distinction, for reasons I shall try to set out.

The economic liberal will argue, as I have said, that relativities do not matter. What matters to the poor person is whether he or she is better off this year than he or she was last year, not whether or not the gap between that person and some other group in society has increased. To take the latter view is in the view of the economic liberal to confuse poverty and inequality. Poverty in the absolute sense, can on this view, be cured by the free market. The trickle-down or echelon-advance effect of the market will be likely over time to increase the absolute living standards of the poor. This is quite consistent with the same free market increasing inequality since by definition inequality does not increase absolute poverty and indeed because of the incentive effects of inequality, may be a condition of dealing with absolute poverty. Tackling inequality in terms of income would on the contrary seem to imply direct state action. Crosland certainly took the view that relative positions matter, and as I have said believed that the fiscal dividends of growth would allow governments to invest in public expenditure which would be to the greatest advantage of the least well off and this would improve the relative position of the worst off. So where does the Labour government stand on this crucial difference between what has historically been a dividing line between social democracy and economic liberalism? Clearly the government rejects equality of outcome, but then so does Crosland. However what seems equally clear is that the government wants to restrict its rhetoric of equality to equality of opportunity and to resist developing any other conception of equality to describe its social goals and to restrict the language of greater social and economic equality to overcoming social exclusion. Social exclusion is seen very much in terms of equality of opportunity and its denial. Government should invest heavily in supply-side measures to improve equality of opportunity in the labour market by investing in employability skills, through the New Deal for the young, the long-term unemployed, and the disabled, by a commitment to improve standards in schools and by developing schemes for life-long learning. All of this is wholly consistent with a Croslandite emphasis on the importance of education to creating genuine equality of opportunity, particularly for those with the worst disadvantages. While they are supply-side measures, rather than outcome measures, they nevertheless go far beyond what an economic liberal would regard as being an appropriate role for the state, both in terms of the degree of intervention in the supply side and in the degree of taxation which has to be raised to finance these measures. Nevertheless the question still remains as to whether these policies will diminish social and economic inequality and whether this question is regarded by the government as important.

In the view of the government, these supply-side measures will increase equality of opportunity and will diminish the sense of social exclusion because, for one thing, they are work oriented. It is clear that one strand in the government's thinking about work oriented policies is that benefit levels for those out of work or the disabled will not be high enough to lead people out of poverty, so the route out of poverty is work and indeed work in a relatively deregulated labour market albeit with a national minimum wage as a floor. So the argument is that work oriented welfare reform will lead people out of poverty and into work and will diminish social exclusion by so doing. The government's supply-side measures, it is argued, will extend the opportunity to work and to acquire the appropriate skills. This is still quite different from saying that an explicit aim of the policy is to improve social and economic equality in any kind of output sense even in Crosland's own complex understanding of that. I would guess that the government's response would be that this is an open question. That is to say, the creation of greater social and economic equality in terms of outcome is not a direct object of policy. The aim is to equip people with the best level of skills they can acquire and then to enter the labour market, a labour market on which no particular constraints will be placed by government in terms of outcome other than for example a higher rate of tax for larger earners and inheritance tax. The degree of inequality of outcome thrown up by the market will then have to be accepted as fair given that starting points of entry into the labour market have been made fairer by the government's supply side employability measures.

If this is so then there is both a similarity and a difference between the government's policy in relation to both economic liberalism and Croslandite social democracy. There is an agreement with the economic liberal in the sense of arguing (however implicitly on the part of the government) that inequality of outcome is not a matter which should be directly addressed by government. There is a difference in that the notion of equality of opportunity in the labour market has been vastly extended by the government's investment in supply-side measures which goes way beyond what the neo-liberal would countenance. There is also a difference from Crosland's version of social democracy in that while the emphasis on equality of opportunity and investing in the skills of the least advantaged is clearly wholly compatible with the Croslandite approach, the reluctance to address the question of whether it is the aim of the Labour government to improve the relative position of the poor (i.e. to decrease inequality) or to improve their absolute position (which is quite compatible with the same levels of inequality as under Margaret Thatcher) marks a fundamental difference since this does seem, historically to be a major dividing line between the neo liberal and the social democratic approach. It may be true, as I have suggested, that a good many of the government's supply-side measures will impact on outcome inequality, but as far as I am aware that, as opposed to diminishing social exclusion, has not been an explicit aim of policy.

Indeed, the government would probably claim on this point that the emphasis upon supply-side measures which marks one of the clear differences between themselves and mid-century social democrats such as Crosland is a result of a modern kind of revisionism which has to take the problems of the global market seriously in a way that Crosland did not. That is to say that the assumptions about the nature of capitalism which Crosland held and which I outlined earlier, and particularly the capacity of national governments to manage economies, have been rendered invalid by the growth of globalisation and that in these circumstances greater outcome equality, even in Crosland's understanding of it, cannot be achieved by direct government action. Rather, people have to be empowered to enter markets, including the labour market, and whether this leads to greater equality of condition is something on which government can have only the most indirect influence through the strength or otherwise of those supply-side measures.

The parallel issue at stake in the discussion of the relationship between New Labour and Croslandite revisionism is the role of benefits. As part of the strategy for diminishing social exclusion, the government is, as I have stressed, investing heavily in work oriented programmes for the young unemployed, the long-term unemployed and the disabled. One of the assumptions here is that tax payers will not pay for benefits which are detached from reciprocity on the part of the recipient and will not pay at a high enough rate to keep all those currently on benefit out of poverty. The aim has therefore been to push a welfare-to-work strategy, to ensure that more people come off benefit, or receive benefits as part of being in work. This in the government's view is the best way of moving people out of poverty and ensuring that individuals discharge the duties of citizenship.

In many respects this runs rather counter to Crosland's approach in that Crosland clearly saw a decent level of benefit as being part of social justice and greater social and economic equality. This was, however, in the context in which unemployment was much lower than it is today and vastly lower than it was in the mid-1980s. It may therefore have been easier to avoid the issue in 1956 because benefits were payable to a smaller group of unemployed people and their dependants and indeed other benefits had not been developed – for example, for the disabled – as opposed to being available through means-tested National Assistance. Consequently, it might have been much more plausible for mid-century social democrats to take a more positive view of benefits since benefits payments accounted for a much smaller proportion of public expenditure. So, when the present government came into office committed to social justice, equality of opportunity and ending social exclusion it had to come to a view about the relationship between benefits and these social ideals and has clearly taken the view that for those able to work, a job is the best way to a better life and the task has been to equip people who have been detached from the labour market with the employability skills to make this a possibility. The real issue of potential contrast between this and a Croslandite approach it seems to me will turn on what benefit levels the government will in the end pay to those who cannot work or are out of work for a long period during an economic down-turn. A Croslandite view would surely be that these levels of payment must be at a level to ensure that poverty is avoided and that people can still have a sense of belonging to society even if they have to live on benefit. While the government said in its 1997 Green Paper on welfare reform that such people will be protected, it has been rather vague in terms of the types of principles which will govern their protection, essentially whether benefits for this group will be at a safety-net level or whether they will be judged in terms of social justice and a commitment to greater equality. The reason why this question is difficult for the government is that given its work oriented strategy for welfare reform it cannot make benefits too generous without sapping the incentive to work. If it were to do this then the government would have to resort to coercion for the able bodied and it will want, so far as it can, to avoid this. So I think that the jury is still out on the issue of the relationship between New Labour and Croslandite revisionism. Crosland believed that means to ends should always be revised in the light of circumstances; the question to which there is not an unambiguous answer as yet is the extent to which New Labour has revised ends as well.

4 Equality – Then and Now*
Gordon Brown

When I was invited to make this contribution on the legacy of Anthony Crosland, I felt both challenged and daunted. Daunted because no one could ever encapsulate his life, his thinking and his achievements – and his sheer humanity – better than Susan Crosland has herself in her remarkable biography. And challenged because Crosland's vision of equality cries out to be restored to its proper place alongside freedom and solidarity in the trinity of socialist values.

When *The Future of Socialism* was published in 1956, it marked a decisive moment in postwar Labour history. No other postwar contribution to Labour thinking has had such an impact and no one who has read it – and his later works – can fail to be impressed by Crosland's intellectual vigour and his clarity of thought or moved by his deep political commitment.

I want to argue that there are three essential elements to Crosland's rich and lasting legacy to Labour: First, he defined equality as the fundamental value that divides the Labour Party from the Conservative Party. You can agree or disagree with Tony Crosland on equality. You may take the view he goes too far or not far enough. You may think he gave too little emphasis to equality for women and that he over-emphasised social and economic equality at the expense of equality in political power. But since 1956, any serious discussion of the politics of equality

---
* Revised and expanded version of platform speech, Memorial meeting (13 February 1997).

must take as its starting point and have as its compass *The Future of Socialism*, his greatest work.

At root, Crosland believed – as I will suggest – in a society in which nobody is deprived of the chance of realising their potential. For him, it was the duty of government not just to attack entrenched privileges that held people back but to vigorously promote equality in life chances and his objective, a classless society, and to do so across the economy, politics and our culture. What he said is – I believe – more relevant than ever today and it is how we apply these egalitarian values to the world of the late 1990s that I want to address my thoughts.

Crosland's second legacy is to make a socialist's central focus his or her essential values, not any particular method of achieving those values. Means may change from time to time, but essential objectives endure. Nationalisation – as he showed in 1956 – was, at best, a means. Equality was his principled objective.

Thirdly, and this is his inspiration for today, he set out to establish a socialist position that was both intellectually rigorous and practically credible for the world as it actually exists. The key to understanding Crosland's legacy for us today is that he was a political thinker who was prepared to grapple with all the day-to-day challenges of practical politics. And in more than 30 years of active politics he never ceased to argue his case or defend his decisions – even as a Cabinet minister – from socialist principle.

There have been left-of-centre politicians who have espoused socialism but fail to meet the test of credibility. There have been those who have presented themselves as credible by abandoning socialism. The real challenge of left-of-centre politics is to be socialist and at the same time credible, a challenge which Crosland met triumphantly, rejecting all sorts of gesture politics along the way. It is the challenge which we in the Labour Party, inspired by Anthony Crosland, fully understand and fully intend to meet.

I want to look at the way the world has changed since Crosland wrote and I want to suggest that far from marginalising the issue of equality, these changes mean that the case for equality is even stronger. I will argue that what happened in Britain over the two decades of Conservative rule – the Tory exaltation of inequality – has made it all the more necessary to make the philosophical case for equality.

I want to translate, into the context of the 1990s, Crosland's idea of democratic equality – a concept that offers more than equality of opportunity, but something other than equality of outcome. And finally, I want to identify the policies that flow from this insight and in particular I will suggest that the only possible starting point today for those who are serious about equality – indeed the pre-condition for tackling inequality – is tackling unemployment.

THE CHANGING CONTEXT FOR EQUALITY

Today's world is, of course, quite different from the world of 1956 in which Crosland first formulated his policies for equality and therefore a new approach will be required, applying our socialist ethics to addressing its inequalities. In 1956 the UK economy was largely a closed economy subject to national controls – import controls, credit controls, demand management by the Treasury – effective within national boundaries. In 1956, under a Conservative government, exchange controls meant that an individual could take just £30 out of the country.

Now we operate in an open, global market in capital and credit where billions of pounds flow in and out of Britain each day. Against this, the old national levers of power which Crosland thought important have less and less influence. And the effect of global competition in goods markets mean that, inevitably, national economic policy must focus less on managing demand and more on supply-side measures necessary for competitiveness – such as promoting long-term investment and education.

When Crosland wrote, physical capital was more important to a firm than its employees, human capital. In 1956 there were less than 50 computers, most of them in Oxford and Cambridge, and now, there are over 10 million computers in Britain. So today we live in an information economy where knowledge is the real source of value and it is skills and ideas that are the assets that matter. The truly indispensable form of capital is intellectual and human capital – not just at the top of a business but throughout the firm.

In 1956 there was one dominant model of employment in the labour market – men working for 40 hours a week for 40 years of their lives in the same job. Today we have a labour market in which almost half the workforce are women, people are working part-time as well as full-time and there are no jobs for life but, at best, a working life of many jobs.

Finally, the most important change of all is that the assumption of full employment, which Crosland could make even in his later works of the 1970s, has gone. In 1956, just 1 per cent of people were unemployed and even in the early 1970s, when Crosland wrote his later works, the figure averaged just 3 per cent. Today, nearly one in five of working age families have nobody in employment.

If Anthony Crosland had been writing today, I believe it is to the issue of workplace generated poverty and inequality that he would have turned his thoughts. I believe that Crosland with his luminous realism would have recognised the need to change in the context of a changing economic world.

In the same way that in 1956 he argued persuasively that socialism did not require a command economy but that, in a national economy, markets could be made to work in the public interest, today in an international economy, he would argue that cooperation in economic policy is essential. Just as Crosland recognised the centrality of growth – and fashioned growth policies for his day – today, in a global economy, supply-side interventions by government are as important as demand management. Just as Crosland defended the mixed economy in the 1950s, making the case for a mix of public and private ownership, so today public and private sectors need to work together in partnership for shared objectives.

In the same way that Crosland argued in 1956 that increased public ownership was not synonymous with the public interest, so today a rise in public spending does not necessarily equate with meeting the public interest. Indeed in 1975, he himself questioned who benefited from spending and expressed concern that 'we have made the painful discovery that a shift from private spending to public spending does not necessarily increase equality.'

In particular, I think he would have recognised that the record since 1979 shows that increased spending does not necessarily increase social justice: that you can tax, spend, borrow... and fail. Indeed, I believe he would have seen that today a new welfare state is needed to bring employment and educational opportunity to those denied it.

So what makes for inequality – and the weapons that we must fashion to achieve greater equality – have changed. But the cause of equality endures. So before I turn in more detail to the question of how we achieve greater equality in the changed world of the 1990s, let us address the fundamental questions central to all that Crosland wrote: What form of equality should we aim for and why?

THE CASE FOR EQUALITY

The Future of Socialism was written at a time when equality was not under attack. Tony Crosland did not therefore feel the need to make the philosophical case for equality. Raymond Plant (see chapter 3 in this volume) has suggested that, by failing to build an intellectual and a popular consensus for Croslandite social democracy, we allowed its collapse in the 1970s. And after 20 years in which New Right ideology which has worshipped inequality has dominated the political landscape, it is now more important then ever that we argue the case for equality from first principles.

Today, we argue for equality not just because of our belief in social justice but also because of our view of what is required for economic success. The starting point is a fundamental belief in the equal worth of every human being. We all have an equal claim to social consideration by virtue of being human. And if every person is to be regarded as of equal worth, all deserve to be given an equal chance in life to fulfil the potential with which they are born.

Crosland wrote of the importance of potential in *Socialism Now*. And in doing so he took issue with the old view – used to justify inequality in educational opportunity – that intelligence was a fixed quantity, something given in limited measure in the genetic make-up of the new-born child. Crosland was right. Intelligence cannot be reduced to a single number in an IQ test taken at the age of 11. People cannot be ranked in a single hierarchy and talent cannot be regarded as fixed. So people should not be written off at 7, 11 or 14 or indeed at any time in their life. It is simply a denial of any belief in equality of opportunity if we assume that there is one type of intelligence, one means of assessing it, only one time when it should be assessed and only one chance of succeeding.

But we have still to act on the consequence of recognising these facts: that people have a richness of potential to be tapped, that their talents take many forms – skills in communication, language, and working with other people as well as analytical intelligence – that these talents can develop over a lifetime, and that to get the best economy we need to get the best out of people's potential. And if we are to allow each person to develop that potential which exists within them, it is clear that we need to develop a more demanding view of equality of opportunity than a one-off equality of opportunity up till age 16.

So I believe that everyone should have the chance to bridge the gap between what they are and what they have it in themselves to become. But what is right on ethical grounds is, in the 1990s, good for the economy too. In our information-age economy, the most important resource of a firm or a country is not its raw materials, or a favourable geographical location, but the skills of the whole workforce. And so prosperity for a company or country can be delivered only if we get the best out of all people, and that cannot happen without continuous and accessible equality of opportunity.

Indeed, I would suggest that Britain's economic weakness is not attributable to a neglect at the top of the educational pyramid, but has arisen because we have given insufficient attention in education and employment policies to the latent and diverse potential of the population as a whole. In the industrial age, the denial of opportunity offended many people but was not necessarily a barrier to the success of the economy. Today, in an economy where skills are the essential means of production, the denial of opportunity has become an unacceptable inefficiency, a barrier to prosperity.

And once we take this view that what matters on ethical and economic grounds is the equal right to realise potential, we reject – as Anthony Crosland did – both an unrealisable equality of outcome and a narrow view of equality of opportunity. Indeed, we reject equality of outcome not because it is too radical but because it is neither desirable nor feasible.

Crosland himself wrote of 'the rent of ability', recognising that incentives for effort are essential in any economic system: greater incomes for some justified by the contribution they make to the society as a whole. Indeed I would go further: pre-determined results imposed, as they would have to be, by a central authority and decided irrespective of work, effort or contribution to the community, is not a socialist dream but other people's nightmare of socialism.

It denies humanity, rather than liberates it. It is to make people something they are not, rather than helping them to make the most of what they can be. What people resent about Britain is not that some people who have worked hard have done well. What angers people is that millions have been denied the opportunity to realise their potential. It is this inequality that must be addressed. Just as we join Crosland in rejecting an unattainable equality of outcome, so we refuse to narrow our horizons to a limited view of equality of opportunity.

There was an old idea of equality of opportunity in which it meant a single chance to get your foot on a narrow ladder, one opportunity at school till 16 followed by an opportunity for 20 per cent to go into higher education. And for millions of people in Britain it has meant that if you missed that chance it was gone forever. It is the equal opportunity only to become unequal: as Crosland wrote 'only a few exceptional individuals hauled out of their class by society's talent scouts, can ever climb'. It is in the words of Tawney the invitation for all to come to dinner in the sure knowledge that circumstances would prevent most people from attending.

Whether done on the basis of birth or academic qualifications, the potential of all is clearly denied when we entrench the privilege of a few. So Crosland correctly concluded that a narrow equality of opportunity was not enough if we were to prevent the entrenchment of unjustifiable privilege, and sought a broader view of equality that complemented rather than conflicted with the importance he attached to personal liberty. He proposed what he called a democratic view of equality – one that sought to prevent the permanent entrenchment of privilege from whatever source it came. This more demanding view of equality of opportunity – democratic equality – had, as he said in *The Conservative Enemy*, 'revolutionary connotations'.

So what, in the 1990s, does this concept of democratic equality mean for me?

First, it demands employment opportunity for all because work is central not just to economic prosperity for Britain but to individual fulfilment. And there must be a permanent duty on government to relentlessly pursue this objective.

Secondly, we must as a society ensure not just a one-off educational opportunity in childhood, but continuing and lifelong educational opportunity for all – second, third, and even fourth chances so that people are not written off if they fail at school and are not left behind by the pace of technological change.

Thirdly, life-long opportunity must be comprehensive, extending beyond education and employment, involving genuine access to culture – and, most importantly, a redistribution of power that offers people real control over the decisions that affect their lives.

While Crosland did write about industrial democracy, he said less about the state or about an equal right to participate in the decisions that affect our lives. In the 1940s people accepted services handed down from the state – for example, housing. They now want to make their own choices over their own lives and rightly see themselves as decision-makers in their own right and they want a government that will enable them to make decisions for themselves and give them power over their lives. So the issue for socialists is not so much about what the state can do for you but about what the state can enable you to do for yourself.

Political reform is central to this: it must enable people to have the chance to participate in decisions that affect them. This is about more than the concept of a classless society, it is about power and therefore about a truly democratic society. Proponents of democratic equality must also – even in a global marketplace – address wealth and income inequalities. I believe that these inequalities can be justified only if they are in the interests of the least fortunate.

Crosland took his stand against inequalities of social status and wealth. He viewed the question of income inequalities as of lesser importance, but he thought that great inequalities of wealth, and particularly inherited wealth, could not be justified as a source of enormous social and economic advantage. But Crosland also saw the distinction between the private ownership of property that simply furthered privilege and the private ownership of property that allowed people control over their lives. So he was ahead of his time on the Left in wanting a more general diffusion of property among the entire population. Indeed, he was right to say in *The Conservative Enemy* that 'If the property is well-distributed, a property-owning democracy is a socialist rather than a conservative ideal.'

Democratic equality means we tackle unjustifiable inequalities, but it also, of course, pre-supposes a guaranteed minimum below which no one should fall. Our minimum standards must include a minimum wage, a tax and benefit system that helps people into work, the best possible level of health and social services for all and the assurance of dignity and security for those who are retired or unable to work through infirmity.

PUTTING EQUALITY INTO PRACTICE

When it came to power, this government was clear that those who support democratic equality must begin by tackling the biggest source of poverty and inequality – unemployment. Employment opportunity for all is hollow when one working age family in five has no one earning a wage. This contrasts with 11.5 per cent in the USA, 15 per cent in Germany and 16 per cent in France. In some inner cities – such as inner-city London or Glasgow for example – there are constituencies where 30 per cent and up to 35 per cent of working-age families have nobody in work.

A far-reaching modernisation of the welfare state was essential, starting with an assault on youth unemployment and long-term unemployment among men and women. So within two months of taking office, the government put in place a massive programme of employment opportunity – a new deal for those excluded from the chance to work. The programme covers the young unemployed and long-term unemployed as well as other groups who have faced permanent exclusion from the labour market – such as single parents and the long-term sick and disabled who want to work.

The new deal for the unemployed is the first building block of the new welfare state of the 1990s. The second element of our modernisation is to re-establish the work ethic at the centre of our welfare system. This involves a reform of the tax and benefit system to make work pay. So in the 1998 budget, the government announced wholesale reform of the tax and benefit system to tackle the unemployment and poverty traps facing low-paid families. This includes a reform of National Insurance and a new Working Families' Tax Credit which will guarantee a minimum income for working families with children. These reforms will be underpinned by the National Minimum Wage.

The third element is to give priority to education. As well as creating work, a modern employment policy must also be about improving people's skills and helping them into new jobs. In the new economy, that will require not just the one-off acquisition of a skill but the continuous acquisition of new skills. So hand in hand with increased employment opportunity goes life-long educational opportunity. Greater educational opportunity will come through an expansion of the numbers going into further and higher education and lifelong learning opportunities will come through our University for Industry, and the creation of Individual Learning Accounts.

So real equality in life chances is what the government seeks. And let me conclude by saying how we are tackling inequalities in opportunities and potential facing women. The days of men-only economic policies – full employment for men, educational equality only for men and a welfare state for men – are over. An economy in which women cannot fulfil themselves in work will be an inefficient economy.

But still nowhere is the gap between the rhetoric of equality of opportunity and the real world of inequality greater than in achieving political, economic and social opportunities for women. Prevented from securing the jobs they want, too often denied childcare which would enable them to gain financial independence, and often debarred even from enjoying a second chance in education, our modernisation of the welfare state will ensure that it becomes far more responsive to the needs of women – allowing them to combine family responsibilities with employment and gain new skills.

Since coming to office, the government has not only established the first national programme of opportunities for work for lone parents, it has for the first time said that employment opportunities will be available not just to the registered unemployed, but also to the partners of the unemployed – mainly women. The government has also invested substantial extra resources in after-school childcare and with the new childcare tax credit in the Working Families' Tax Credit, we are tackling the problem of the affordability of childcare. And with extra resources provided for child benefit, the government is supporting all families with children. Taken together, these measures are the first steps to providing a genuine chance for women to balance work and family responsibilities

So the government is putting forward a radical agenda for equal opportunity. It is a far-reaching conception of equal opportunity in which we believe, a modern conception for the modern world. And it tackles the causes of inequality at the root – dealing not simply with the consequences of poverty but addressing the causes – unemployment and low skills.

CONCLUSION

I would argue that our commitment to equality is as strong as ever. We are applying it, however, in the new circumstances we face. That means never being diverted from our egalitarian ends, but being aware that policies may change to take account of changed times. So our policies are credible because we build from a platform of stability on tax, spending and borrowing.

There is no alternative to this iron commitment. But it is socialist because we are talking about toughness for a purpose – an egalitarian purpose:

- Giving unemployed people opportunities currently denied to them.
- Making work pay for all families.
- Lifelong educational opportunities for everyone to acquire new skills.

I have outlined what I see as some of the egalitarian policies of the 1990s. This is the agenda we are pursuing in government. And I hope and believe it is an agenda which does justice to Tony Crosland's intellectual and political memory.

5 Anthony Crosland and Socialism*
Michael Young

> Our society will look quite different when we have carried through the changes... and the whole argument will then need to be re-stated and thought out afresh, by a younger generation than mine.
> (C.A.R. Crosland, *The Future of Socialism*, 1956)

Looking back on it, what was it that made Crosland's death a public as well as a private tragedy? He had not made his mark as a public personality, like Bevan or Churchill or even 'Fight, Fight, and Fight Again' Gaitskell. He had not much of the actor about him, no flamboyance on the platform or in the studio. But he was cut down in full stature rather than when stumbling about in death's anteroom. Like a much younger man, he was still climbing, faster indeed than at any other period of his life, on the way to the Treasury (where any decisions that can be taken about moves towards greater fiscal equality presumably are).

Crosland was a man of words and a man of action, too. He was the greatest socialist revisionist of his time, and perhaps something of that came through to a wider public when it was not a slur to be an intellectual.

He was not a 'lateral' thinker. I rarely heard him jump to a sharp judgement on a subject he had not already got up. If someone had not really studied something, he (especially if he was an intellectual) did not have an opinion worth listening to. He should

---
* Written for this volume.

do his homework instead of spouting. Crosland was a 'vertical' thinker, a marvellously deep one, who drilled down into a subject with unflagging force until he was at last able to come up with the ore of his own conclusions. I was quite often frightened by this intellectual power and the scornfulness it could sometimes generate. I usually tried, when I wanted his opinion on something I was doing, to fortify my own arguments with special care lest he scatter them all with his hammer counts of firstlies, secondlies, and thirdlies. I did this when I was writing *The Chipped White Cups of Dover* (1960), a pamphlet advocating a new Consumers' Party. For once I did not need to fear. He thought it 'amusing'. Anything amusing had a special dispensation of tolerance. He commented in detail on the margins of two drafts of it in his meticulous handwriting. Earlier, I discussed with him at length the general ideas behind my book on *The Rise of the Meritocracy* (1958), but I did not dare show him a draft at all in case, not being given that dispensation, it did not stand up to his withering scrutiny.

But for almost all the time I knew him I was aware of him, if at a little distance, not as one or other, intellectual or politician, so much as both together, in the form of a friend. His ability to blend the two was his rarest quality. He did it by using that same mental power to work out his own plans of action both on the grand and the small scale. He took hardly anything for granted. Instead, like a researcher, he went back to basic sources; and then, unlike a researcher, worked his way through to conclusions which were for action, which is perhaps why he was sometimes almost over-lucid in the analysis which led up to them. For an optimist, there had to be an answer. But if one was to be found he never took it on anyone's authority except his own. His voice carried conviction because it was always the voice of someone thinking out his position for himself.

Traditional socialism was largely concerned with the evils of traditional capitalism, and with the need for its overthrow. But today traditional capitalism has been reformed and modified almost out of existence, and it is with a quite different form of society that socialists must now concern themselves.

Crosland's grand plan was set out in *The Future of Socialism*, published in 1956, before he embarked on the most active part of his political career. It turned out the most important book on socialism for 25 years. It still seems remarkable, for someone who wanted to succeed in a Labour Party which had always been split between its belief in an equality which is more felt than thought and its day-to-day reformist pragmatism which is more thought than felt. He tried to connect action to belief, which meant doing the almost unpardonable (at the time) by wryly spelling out the success of postwar capitalism – full employment, economic growth, rising standards of life. 'The first miners' Car Rally was recently held in Yorkshire... Half the population now leave home for at least a week's annual holiday.'

Maynard Keynes in the background seemed just as significant for the revisionist thesis as Clem Attlee in the foreground. The change since the 1930s meant that there was no need to 'abolish private ownership of the means of production'. But if the methods had altered there was still a very great deal to be done to achieve the main end of socialism which has in the 1990s sadly seemed to pale away: greater social and economic equality. Much of Crosland's book is about how to do it.

Very little in of *The Future Socialism* seems wrong to me, and much of it so contemporary that only the passing references to Lady Docker, to the power of the Beaverbrook Press, or to Karen Horney,[1] put one back into period. The weaknesses are of omission

– because society has again changed so much in two decades. Crosland in *Socialism Now* (1974) admitted his own disappointment about the economic growth which, in his view, was one essential key to equality; and he accepted the arrival of environmental politics. Perhaps his main omission was that he had so little to say about ways of 'redistributing' or 'equalising' the power of the state and other bureaucracies like the trade unions. After recognising the problem well enough in *The Future of Socialism*, he then largely left it alone. He was for the rest of his life so busy using that power to advance equality, and also to promote freedom, that he did not have much time to think about the right treatment of the one privilege which he needed for everything else he did. The forms of equality had been fostered only by concentrating more power in the state.

But if the intellectual force was not used to tackle that dilemma, it was for every particular issue which he encountered when in office. He must have driven hundreds of British civil servants half-mad by refusing to accept what they said until he had personally burrowed into it in depth and convinced himself of the policy needed.

I was close to him on only one of those issues. In 1963 he persuaded me (indeed he shamed me, as one brought up in a family of Plymouth Brethren could do so well) into acting as a mini-Crosland to his Gaitskell. I more or less gave up everything else to work nearly full-time for six months on 'The Problem of the Public Schools', as secretary to a Fabian committee of which he was Chairman and Shirley Williams a member. There was so much detail in the final report I wrote about the politics of it all that I did not publish for fear of embarrassing a future Labour Minister of Education, and in the hope, if the Minister took up the proposals, that he or she would present them as his own. But when he was that Minister I could not persuade him to act because (naturally enough, in retrospect) I could not persuade him that the reform of the public schools was more important than the improvement of ordinary secondary schools on comprehensive lines, or the introduction of the binary system of higher education. Nor would he agree to set up a Commission of Enquiry on the subject until he had had time to go into the subject once again himself; and when the Public Schools Commission did come it was too late for anything to be done within that Parliament. In this instance, I was the loser. Each time I argued for more priority for reforming the public schools I knew he had the stronger case (and also, grudgingly, that if I had been him and he me, he would probably have persuaded me).

> Now the time has come for a reaction: for a greater emphasis on private life, on freedom and dissent, on culture, beauty, leisure, and even frivolity. Total abstinence and a good filing system are not now the right sign-posts to the socialist Utopia; or at least, if they are, some of us will fall by the wayside.

This was the new element in his socialism. A good society would be one in which people would have *more fun* as well as being more equal, perhaps partly because they would be able to be more amused by each other if the 'barrier of class' were removed. Though an inhibited man himself, he certainly did not put barriers round his own personality. He was loveable because he did not mind whether he was loved or not. He was always so fully himself on the hundreds of occasions I met him since 1945, without humbug but finding bitingly amusing the humbug in others. He brought the sense of fun to the life he shared with his marvellous wife, Susan, to whom I remain devoted.

That bit of revisionist socialism he lived out himself.

Note

1. Lady Docker was a socialite renowned for her extravagent lifestyle; Lord Beaverbrook was a powerful right-wing newspaper proprietor and former Tory politician who owned the *Daily Express*, *Sunday Express* and *Evening Standard*; Karen Horney was a famous psychoanalyst best known for her book *New Ways in Psychoanalysis*. (*Editor's Note*.)

Part II
Ministerial Record

6 Crosland as a Minister*
Roy Hattersley

Like most provincial politicians of my generation, I discovered Tony Crosland through *The Future of Socialism*. I no longer recall what sort of man I imagined him to be. But, despite the famous passage about the limited attraction of abstinence and good filing systems, I certainly thought of him as an ascetic. The mistake was reinforced when Hugh Gaitskell came to Sheffield to lay the foundation stone for a block of municipal flats. 'Tony', he told the assembled civic dignitaries over lunch, 'has agreed to write the report of the co-operative movement.' He took it for granted that we all knew which Tony he meant. Fred Mulley – Member of Parliament for the constituency in which the new housing development was to be built – whispered in my ear that it was Crosland, not Benn or Greenwood. It confirmed my view that the classic restatement of democratic socialist values had been written by a serious-minded academic.

In a sense, my judgement was correct. Crosland was one of the most serious politicians I have ever met. 'Frivolous' was, for him, a term of abuse. But even as Foreign Secretary – an office which is usually thought to be synonymous with gravitas – he needed, from time to time, to hide his stern commitment to clear thinking and decisive action behind a protective shield of flippancy. Some time before 1959 – when I was candidate in safe Conservative Sutton Coldfield – Ian Mikardo spoke for me at a public meeting. During the supper which followed, Mikardo denounced

---
* Written for this volume.

Crosland for a speech which he had made opposing the nationalisation of the aerospace industry. It had included the ironic aside, 'after all we only beat three world records last week'. Mikardo was not a man to tolerate jokes about public ownership. 'Oxford Union stuff', he said. 'That boy will never make a minister.'

In 1964, Crosland became Minister of State in George Brown's Department of Economic Affairs. He was also, in effect, Economic Secretary to Jim Callaghan at the Treasury. It is now almost universally agreed that the new government should have faced the inherited economic crisis by an immediate devaluation. Callaghan, and to a lesser extent Brown, believed that a change in the pound – dollar parity would provide only a brief respite to the chronic balance of payments problem. Harold Wilson ruled it out for the essentially political reason that Labour – having devalued under Stafford Cripps 15 years before – could not afford to make a habit of reducing the value of the pound. It was Tony Crosland who argued convincingly and realistically – though, unhappily, unsuccessfully – that devaluation was right as well as unavoidable and that it was better for the government to make a voluntary and managed adjustment to the exchange rate than to have one forced upon it. If Crosland's advice had been accepted, the history of the 1960s might well have been changed.

Crosland's role as intermediary between the Treasury and Department of Economic Affairs – rival ministries which Harold Wilson thought would produce 'creative tension" – was described by Ted Heath in the House of Commons as what the French called "a dumbbell arrangement'. He added that there was no doubt about who was the belle between the two dumb Cabinet Ministers. Naturally the weak joke brought the House down – the Commons is like that. But the spontaneity of the laughter was a confirmation that

Members thought of Tony Crosland as a star. Unfortunately, he did not always live up to his billing. His speech, at the end of the debate, concentrated exclusively on something called Operation Neptune – a plan to combat coast erosion which was barely relevant to the day's business. But the scheme had caught Crosland's imagination. So he talked about it. Tony Crosland was like that. During his first year as Foreign Secretary, he was host to a lunch for Henry Kissinger in the Banqueting Hall in Westminster. Before he proposed the toasts to the Queen, to the President of the USA and to the 'heads of other states here represented', he insisted on the assembled company drinking to Inigo Jones, the architect of the building.

But Crosland always confined his indiscipline to minor matters. On great issues of policy he was what a more recent generation would call 'firmly focused'. Indeed when he was in pursuit of a new idea, or the better application of an old one, he was impossible to divert from his chosen path. Indeed, my first real conversation with him was the result of his determination to discuss education with me, whether I liked it or not. We had already met at an institution called The 1963 Club – an organisation which dined in memory of Hugh Gaitskell. But there had been no time for the acquaintance to develop. Crosland had left during the second course, complaining that he was bored by the assembled company's constant criticisms of Harold Wilson. He added, as he passed through the door, that it was demeaning constantly to talk about a rebellion without ever having the slightest intention to mount one. As I was to discover when we became friends, talk without action always irritated him.

The real first meeting took place in the Division Lobby of the House of Commons. I was asking Dick Crossman about a visit he proposed to make (as Housing Minister) to Birmingham, when Tony asked me to spare him moment. I replied, 'Of course, Mr Crosland!' So the first few minutes of our conversation were taken up with a cross-examination about why I was so formal with him when I treated other Cabinet ministers with proper disrespect. Dissatisfied with my explanation, he moved on to the topic he had originally intended to discuss with me.

After Patrick Gordon Walker's double defeat – first in the 'nigger for a neighbour' campaign in Smethwick in the 1964 general election and then at the Leyton by-election in January 1965 after a parliamentary vacancy had been created for him – Michael Stewart had been promoted from Secretary of State for Education and Science to Foreign Secretary. Roy Jenkins had been offered Education, but had chosen to stay at Aviation, outside the Cabinet. Tony Crosland, Education Secretary by intellect and instinct, had been Harold Wilson's second choice. That night, as we voted, he wanted to talk to me about why Sheffield had come so belatedly to comprehensive education. On the following evening there was a 'running three-line whip' which confined us all to the House. We would – it was a statement, not an invitation – have dinner together in the Members' Dining Room.

I was reluctant to refuse. But my father was in London and, on the following day, I was booked to have dinner in the Strangers' Dining Room with him. I told Crosland of my problem, hoping that he would accept my apology and understand that I would have had dinner with him if it had been possible. He understood, but he did not accept. We would all have dinner together. It was, he said, a unique opportunity. For he knew that my father was a major figure in local government. It in fact was my mother who was city councillor, committee chairman and future Lord Mayor of Sheffield. But, in that mood, there was no arguing with Tony. Reluctantly – and riddled with something that can only be described as stage fright – my father and I had dinner with the Secretary of State for Education and Science. Tony ignored me completely and asked my father – a very junior councillor who had only stood for election because it was the only way of spending his retirement with my mother – complicated questions about the reorganisation of Sheffield secondary schools. That was the moment when my father felt that he had become somebody in the Labour movement. Five years later, when he became a governor at Sheffield Polytechnic, he would tell anybody who would listen that he knew Tony Crosland, the inventor of the new 'binary system' of higher education.

Crosland inherited the Department of Education at a time when the national tide was flowing strongly towards the end of 11+ selection. Edward Boyle – Macmillan's last Education Minister – certainly accepted the inevitability and probably the benefit of the comprehensive revolution. By the end of his period of office, 96 of the 140 local education authorities had applied to end selection. The Labour government promised to accelerate that process. Within a few months of taking office, the sudden necessity to reshuffle the government brought to the Department of Education and Science (as it had been renamed) the ideal Secretary of State to force the pace. Anthony Crosland's strength – tragically, almost unique in the Labour Party after the defeat of the Attlee government – was absolute and total confidence in the superiority of egalitarian socialism over all other philosophies. In *The Future of Socialism* he had written that 'the school system of Britain remains the most divisive, unjust and wasteful of all aspects of social equality'. At the DES he determined to do what he could to right that wrong. Circular 10/65 – which requested local education authorities to end 11+ selection – had been drafted before his arrival. He decided not to replace 'request' with 'require' in the hope that the reform, being voluntary, would survive a change of government. And so it turned out. Between 1970 and 1974, far from reversing the Crosland policy, Margaret Thatcher enthusiastically carried it on. But Crosland did introduce an element of coercion. After 1966, permission for new secondary school building was granted only to authorities which were, in the jargon of the day, 'going comprehensive'.

Each 'reorganisation plan' had to be submitted, individually, to the Secretary of State who – before approving or dismissing it – was obliged to hear objections. That task was inevitably delegated to a Minister of State – in Crosland's case, Shirley Williams. The Secretary of State was regularly infuriated by the meticulous care with which his junior minister examined every reservation and doubt. I remember him saying that whenever a Townswomen's Guild 'wanted to quibble about a catchment area', the whole scheme was postponed for three months. Crosland's conviction about the ideological importance of comprehensive education made him impatient. Impatience is a major asset in a minister.

In August 1967, Crosland was 'promoted' to President of the Board of Trade. His successor, under pressure from the Treasury, abandoned plans to increase the school leaving age to 16 – though the retreat was carried in the Cabinet by only a single vote. Crosland himself voted with the minority. But before his move from Curzon Street to Victoria, he introduced the 'binary system' – the creation of a two-tier higher education sector in which polytechnics (under the control of local authorities and awarding their own degrees) existed side by side with independent universities. The intention was to create institutions which took technological education seriously and 'to move away from the snobbish caste-ridden hierarchical obsession with university status'. If Crosland hoped for parity of esteem in higher education, he was disappointed, and Lord Robbins, speaking in the House of Lords, was entitled to express his surprise that the man who had wanted to unify secondary education should want to divide the higher education sector. But he might well have added that Crosland had come very near to making the central aspiration of his report a practical reality. The expansion of the universities, the creation of degree-awarding polytechnics and the easier availability of maintenance grants meant that there were more students in higher education than ever before.

The 'achievement' for which Crosland's years at the DES will be remembered was, paradoxically, the Open University, an innovation for which he had no great enthusiasm and would have gladly sacrificed if the money it cost could have been switched to pre-school education. The idea – pioneered by Michael Young, one of Crosland's many occasional gurus – was built on a combination of the British correspondence course and the US experiment in education by television. Harold Wilson was so enthusiastic for a 'University of the Air' that the Treasury was never able to cut the infant institution's budget. There is little doubt that Crosland did not regard it as either his greatest spending priority or his greatest ministerial achievement.

At the end of Wilson's first administration, Tony Crosland became Minister of Housing and Local Government, with the task of amalgamating all the 'Environment Departments' into the giant ministry which he was to head when Labour was re-elected in 1974. In that new Department, he made a classical error of constructing a memorable soundbite. Although it captured the mood of the moment, its underlying theme did not represent his view. The half-hearted aphorism haunted him and his successors for the next 20 years. Speaking to local councillors about that year's

Rate Support Grant – the Treasury's subsidy to local government – he told them: 'The party's over.'

Crosland – an advocate of government action and the spending which inevitably follows – suddenly became the prophet of fiscal prudence. 'Even Tony Crosland thinks the government is spending too much', the new monetarists argued and went on to claim that the implication of his phrase was that local government was spending money which could better be left to fructify in the pockets of ratepayers. Whatever Crosland meant at the time of his meeting, his belief in the necessity for high levels of public expenditure remained, in principle, undimmed. Throughout the IMF crisis of 1976, Crosland was the one consistent voice which cogently argued that the government must preserve as much of its public spending programme as was possible.

Tony Crosland became Foreign Secretary in the spring of 1976 after Jim Callaghan succeeded Harold Wilson as Prime Minister. There was no doubt that he wanted the Treasury – as he had wanted it during the first Wilson government. But he applied himself to the Foreign Office with genuine and immense enthusiasm. The flippancy – that hid the seriousness of purpose – remained. When, at his first meeting with the Council of Ministers of the European Community, he heard that a junior minister at the previous meeting had been attacked for suggesting a phrase in a communiqué which, according to the French Foreign Minister, 'offended Cartesian logic', he added a postscript to his response to the President's speech of welcome. 'And let us hear no more about Descartes. I know more about him than anyone here.'

Crosland took to the arcane procedures of the then European Community far more readily than his critics would have anticipated. He was not by intellect or inclination a passionate European. Indeed in the great House of Commons European vote in 1971, he actually abstained. But he realised that the Community was the vehicle through which Britain could both prosper and increase its influence throughout the world. In consequence, he chaired the six months of British Presidency, which began in January 1977, with far more verve than anyone expected. But no one could claim that he would have been satisfied with the Foreign Office alone. He certainly could not accept the conventions of that great office of state. The Prime Minister was regularly irritated by the Foreign Secretary's habit of dealing with 'Foreign Affairs' – traditionally the third item on the Thursday Cabinet agenda – with a terse 'Nothing to report'.

Yet, when he regarded an issue as worth his time and attention, Crosland applied himself to it with immense determination. The fishing dispute between Iceland and the UK had dragged on for two years before Crosland became Foreign Secretary and, as well as embittering relations between two friendly nations, had put at risk the lives of British fishermen whose 'warps' (the lines by which nets were attached to their boats) were cut by Icelandic gunboats. Crosland, a Grimsby MP, certainly thought of himself as the fishermen's friend. But he also thought that the 'Cod War' was supremely silly. The Danish Foreign Minister offered to intervene to produce a negotiated settlement. At a Council of Europe meeting in Copenhagen, Crosland – uninvited – visited the intermediary's hotel and insisted that a deal be worked out there and then.

The enthusiasm to manage the economy persisted. So did his belief in the need to build a more equal society and the important part which was played in that process by redistributive taxation and high levels of public expenditure. Fate – as well as instinct and intellect – seemed to have prepared him to oppose what has come to be called 'the IMF crisis'. In the autumn of 1976, only a few months after Crosland became Foreign Secretary, the government concluded that, to avoid an unacceptable run on sterling, the Public Sector Borrowing Requirement (PSBR) would have to be reduced from 12 million to 9 million pounds.

Crosland's first instinct was that the cuts were not necessary – no more than a guess but one which, in the event, turned out to be true. The PSBR, a notoriously difficult figure to calculate, was already lower than the figure to which the government felt it had to be reduced. When the Chancellor resisted his pleas to risk the consequences of making no cuts, Crosland argued with immense force that everything possible should be done to protect both employment and public services. In even that endeavour he was only marginally successful. After 42 days of crisis and six special Cabinet meetings, the Prime Minister told him – on a plane during the return to Britain from a European summit – that the time had come to resolve the issue. The next day, Jim Callaghan himself would endorse the Chancellor's austerity package. Crosland thought that loyalty required him to do the same.

It was the IMF crisis of 1976 that began to turn the tide of Labour Party opinion away from high levels of public expenditure, and therefore perhaps marks the turning point in the ideology of British democratic socialism. Had Crosland lived, he would have undoubtedly wanted to reassert the crucial necessity of economic redistribution. As it is, egalitarian socialism died with him.

7 Education Secretary*
Christopher Price

THE ACCIDENTAL MINISTER

Charles Anthony Raven Crosland became Secretary of State for Education and Science in February 1965; it was not a particularly sought-after post in Labour circles. No previous Labour Minister had succeeded in having much effect on the English education system. Sir Charles Trevelyan in the 1920s had all his plans destroyed by the Roman Catholic hierarchy; Ellen Wilkinson, in 1945, was ill for much of the 18 months in which she held the job; George Tomlinson, Wilkinson's successor, was pawn of his civil servants; while Crosland's immediate predecessor, Michael Stewart, had turned out to be quite exceptionally timid in his mere 12 weeks of office. Probably the best model he had was Rab Butler, Minister of Education throughout the Second world War and a Conservative. Butler had done more to eliminate educational class divisions than any Labour Minister of Education.

Crosland arrived in the job by accident. Patrick Gordon Walker, who had been appointed Foreign Secretary (somewhat rashly) by Wilson in spite of the fact that he had *lost* a safe Labour seat at Smethwick in the 1964 general election, had just succeeded in losing a second one (at Leyton) in an artificially contrived by-election three months later. So a cabinet reshuffle became necessary; Stewart became Foreign Secretary and Crosland Minister of Education.

In both political and personal terms it was a distinct political risk for Wilson to appoint Crosland. The

---
* Written for this volume.

cabinet was already top-heavy with devotees of the Right and Crosland had a 'reputation'. He was still dogged by a fatal mixture of images which dated back to his early raffish behaviour; between his marriages in the late 1950s, his *machiste* conduct at Fabian Summer Schools had become legendary; while his spaniel-like devotion to Hugh Gaitskell had induced an almost libellous profile in the *New Statesman* entitled 'Mr Gaitskell's Ganymede', alongside a sinuous and androgynous cartoon. Vicky (the cartoonist) had Tony to perfection – decadent talent in a double breasted suit. He was seen by his puritan enemies (on the Left and the Right) as both playboy and office boy. Becoming Secretary of State for Education gave him a chance of proving his mettle.

POLITICAL STYLE

Crosland inherited an English school and university system which had developed out of a complicated amalgam of religious foundations, class and imperialism. It was still deeply hierarchical and Crosland was determined to transform it. Although he had never 'run' anything before in his life, he rapidly turned out to be a natural political leader. He never believed that 'the devil was in the detail' and did not get bogged down in minutiae or insoluble problems. He concentrated on one primary objective – how to reduce the historical divisions in the school and college system in order to reduce such divisions in society. He did not need models from the past because he had spent the past 10 years thinking and writing about how society might be transformed in the future.

Crosland was unique among Labour politicians in having thought through the philosophical basis of Labour policy and written a book about it – the *Future of Socialism* - which he saw as a work of Marxist economic revisionism; in fact it was more a personal tract – seeking somehow to reconcile his own obsessions of equality, class and socialism. Although he had achieved a fellowship at Trinity College, Oxford (still today one of the most elitist institutions in Britain) he was quite unfazed by the peculiarly nasty environment of Oxford academic arrogance in which he worked; and, unlike his much more successful ministerial rival, Roy Jenkins, was never seduced by the social and material charms of the English upper classes. The *Future of Socialism* was full of pleas for society to become more 'gay' (in its 1950s' sense); but Crosland's intensely serious intellectual purpose always sat perfectly easily with his determination that life should be more fun. By 1965 he had come to believe that a Labour government could 'square the equality' circle in his own lifetime. In this sense, quite unlike others on the 'Right' of the Labour party, he was an instinctive nonconformist and a true revisionist (or as Blair might put it, a modernist); his nonconformity emerged from his harsh and stifling Plymouth Brethren pedigree; his revisionism from his willingness to revisit the established doctrines of the Left.

His unique combination of intellectuality, arrogance and sheer love of life made for a style which commanded assent amongst his acolytes and opponents alike. Its effect on me, as his PPS, is reflected in something I wrote many years later around an incident at a meeting of University Vice Chancellors early in 1967:

> Crosland affronted the vice chancellors still further at the end of 1966 by forcing them to charge higher fees to overseas students. The move led to an ill-tempered meeting between Tony and the vice chancellors. Sir Douglas Logan, the Principal of London University and a man of humble origins, was deeply upset by the supercilious drawl Tony

would always put on when he wanted to get the upper hand over those he thought were trying to patronise him. Logan gave as good as he got, venting his spleen. London University was the Athens of the British Empire and it was a scandal that it should have this form of financial discrimination forced upon it. Tony continued to drawl back in summing up. It was the beginning of years of bad blood between government and universities. Tony's cavalier demeanour could appear as hurtful superiority to folk from less confident backgrounds; and he never understood that some academics, including Sir Douglas, were not nearly as confident as their place and office appeared to make them in coping with his particular brand of senior common room repartee.

To me Tony's socialist arrogance was his most endearing characteristic. He insisted that it was only the mighty whom he ever put down from their seats and made a principle of being gentle and sympathetic to shy questioners at public meetings. It was a characteristic which his wife Susan also loved. The final paragraph of her biography of him describes a scene in the fishing town of Grimsby, which Crosland had represented and had remained loyal to Labour against all the odds at the by-election after he died; a *Times* editorial had dismissed the result as 'puzzling' since a personal regard for a man like Mr Crosland could have played no part in it.

'"Sod the patronising buggers," said one of the by-election workers in Grimsby's Labour Party office where they were handing round the national press reports of their "shock" win. He flung *The Times* to the floor. 'It's people like the fancy pants boys who wrote that – who think they're so bloody superior – who couldn't understand Tony. My God it was a pleasure to watch him put them down". He started to cry. That being unmanly, he left the crowded office and went down the narrow steep steps to the door which leads outside.'

A more sober view of this comes in *The Politics of Education*, a book of interviews with Crosland (and Sir Edward Boyle) conducted by Maurice Kogan in 1970. Asked what a minister can actually do, Crosland admits it is harder for him to sum up his style than a properly objective critic, but then goes on:

> I think the prime achievement was a matter of morale and impetus. A minister has the duty – indeed he alone can fulfil this duty – of trying to create a sense of impetus, of things moving, of deep concern for education, a sense that we are all actively working towards a goal of better education, a sense of positive partnership between government, local authorities and teachers. I would like to think ... that while I was there we succeeded in creating this sense of movement and impetus, so contributing to a higher morale in the whole service.

This concentration on *impetus* led him to prioritise long-term strategic objectives which he knew would take a long time to mature. Talking to Maurice Kogan again:

> In your two years you can certainly lay down long term objectives in the central fields – secondary reorganisation, the pattern of higher education, teacher supply, the organisation of science – though of course you will seldom see them finally achieved.

He would demote what he saw as irrelevant, non-urgent issues with a characteristic wave of the hand. He quotes (against himself, again in the Kogan interview) a passage from his wife Susan's diary as an example of this:

Tony came home tonight with Red Box no. 3. 'If I had more ministers and more time it would be fun. It's not now.' Evidently a lengthy day of X talking in Cabinet and fresh papers piling up as fast as earlier ones are dealt with. Advent of Jennie Lee clearly going to be an additional complication. 'To tell you the truth, I'm not frightfully interested in the Arts at this moment in time.' I reminded him that last week he told me after a dinner with vice-chancellors all asking for more money 'To tell you the truth I'm not frightfully interested in the universities at this moment.' And a week before when Vaizey, etc. etc., had all accosted him on the subject of the public schools: 'If the truth be known, I'm not frightfully interested in the public schools at this moment.' He denies he ever said it but he did – probably because 1. he has an extravagant mode of speech, 2. his powers of concentration are extreme (and can be exclusive), and 3. in fact he does think that only teacher supply and the comprehensive issue deserve priority at the moment.

He saw himself as cool, systematic, strategic and prioritising; but that was not how he came over to the education world. There, he was a cavalier among roundheads; his *chutzpah* and political confidence were so infectious that they provided the impetus to the policies he saw as so essential; and side by side with his certainty and even arrogance about the requirements of the *political* task in front of him – the reshaping of education and society – was a genuine humility about his lack of knowledge of the detail of the state education system and a voracious appetite for consultation. After the 1966 general election I saw a lot of this. Another extract from my personal impressions:

Within days of my arrival in London [after becoming an MP] I was offered a real job. Tony Crosland, the Secretary of State for Education and Science would like me to come and see him. I duly appeared. 'Would I be his Parliamentary Private Secretary?' He had been in the job for little more than a year and wanted a PPS who knew something about local authorities and comprehensive education. He had one already, an elderly trade unionist called Cyril Bence, whom he had inherited from his predecessor; Cyril was a canny general adviser but he had no taste for detail, still less for the detail of education policy. It came as a relief to be offered typecast me as a orthodox supporter of the Right. Luckily Crosland had a clear idea of what he wanted from a PPS; most ministers kept their Parliamentary Private Secretaries off the ministry premises and simply used them for dogsbody duties when they were answering questions in the House or speaking in debates: running little errands for the ministers of state, as Gilbert and Sullivan had it. Tony wanted me in the engine room. So the job also took me out of the Westminster hothouse to the Ministry in Curzon Street, a delightfully seedy building next to MI5 in what was then London's premier red light district.

Tony wanted me in the Ministry because he believed in diluting his civil servants' advice with that of outsiders. He had signed up Professor 'Chelly' Halsey to help with social aspects and Ian Byatt for economics. He used intelligent and sympathetic academics as a foil to his equally intelligent but less sympathetic civil servants. He would sit there at the head of the table, puffing a cigar and taking the various points, calling on each of us to come in on cue and then sum up, always the rational being and always getting his way but never banging the table to get it. He would divide and rule his functionaries, winning many over to be as devoted followers as his own advisers.

Strategic meetings took place at his house in Lansdowne Road, to which an outer circle of dons and chief education officers would also be invited; they acted often as pre-meetings to a crucial one in the ministry the following week; only when some sort of line emerged would the whisky come out and the conversation would be allowed to become general and edge towards political gossip.

These discussions with Tony Crosland in the chair had an authentic music of their own which seduced teachers, civil servants, chief education officers, and even the dour uncompromising Presbyterian Scot, Sir William Alexander who, as Secretary of the Association of Education Committees, believed he had a divine right to censor any proposed change in the English educational system.

COMPREHENSIVE SCHOOLS AND THE ABOLITION OF THE 11 +

When Crosland arrived at the Department, his predecessor, Michael Stewart, had been considering the imposition of comprehensive education by decree – and even imposing a single type of institution, the 11–18 comprehensive secondary school. Crosland substituted Stewart's centralist policy with one of allowing comprehensive schools to develop; he also introduced an element – then quite new – of what has since become known as spin doctoring:

> I was particularly wrapped up with the public relations elements of the comprehensive policy. A year earlier, Tony had issued a circular[1] requesting, rather than requiring, local authorities to prepare comprehensive plans. We were thus able to insist that the principle of local autonomy was unscathed. It was also true that the eleven plus examination

was violently unpopular with parents; the post war baby boom youngsters were increasingly coming up to the age of 11 and most local councils were not providing enough places to satisfy parental grammar school aspirations; in many areas, hardly one in 12 children had the chance of passing the 11 plus, sometimes because the councillors were parsimonious but mostly because received Burtian wisdom had it that 12 to 15 per cent of each cohort of children was about right.

A few Conservative county councils, like Cambridgeshire and Leicestershire, under two inspired chief education officers, Henry Morris and Stuart Mason, had pioneered the comprehensive idea long before it became part of Labour's official ideology; the landowners who chaired these rural education committees sent their own male offspring to feepaying public schools and were usually happy to fall in with an idea that appeared to save money by avoiding the need for new grammar schools; and sometimes saved them having to send their daughters to fee paying schools. By now a large number of both Labour county boroughs and Conservative county councils were experimenting with plans for one or two comprehensives; they knew the cash would be readily forthcoming for such projects. All over Britain new comprehensives began to spring up alongside the grammar schools.

In the Department of Education, we followed two particular rules. Our language concentrated on ditching the thoroughly unpopular 11 plus exam; and we put out a series of press releases each time we gave permission for any new planned but as yet unbuilt, comprehensive school. 'Shropshire goes with the comprehensive tide'; 'Devonshire opts for all-in schools'. (Because most of the popular papers had an editorial ban on all four syllable words, 'all-in' had become a code for comprehensive.) In most cases the county concerned was simply putting a speculative toe in the comprehensive pool. But the press release created the impression of a snowballing tide of educational change to the point where such a snowball actually began to roll on for the next ten years – right through Mrs Thatcher's reign as Secretary of State for Education in the early 1970s.

Crucial in all this was the department's control over capital spending. All counties needed permission to build new secondary schools to keep up with the post war shift of population out of the cities; but they could only get that permission if they made noises about ending their 11 plus. The appropriate noises usually developed into decisive action when they saw how popular their policies were. The only local councils that could afford not to were small suburban boroughs, like Kingston on Thames. Their defiance proved our point. They were judged to be stick-in-the-mud reactionaries.

Crosland, in many ways, was lucky. The ground had been prepared and the atmosphere was right. In 1944 Rab Butler had ensured that his Education Act paved the way for the abolition of selection at the age of 11; Sir Edward Boyle had been quietly encouraging comprehensive schemes in the early 1960s; 11 + selection (whether by examination or otherwise) was bitterly unpopular, especially in the new burgeoning middle-class estates where they were not enough grammar school places to satisfy the needs of aspirant parents. The momentum for the abolition of selection could not have gathered strength as it did had there not been genuine popular demand for it.

Over the 30 years which followed his tenure of the Education Ministry, the comprehensive idea survived wave after wave of attacks – from the Black Papers; from Mrs Thatcher's reign as minister when against her instincts she was constrained to close hundreds of grammar schools because the comprehensive tide was so strong; from James Callaghan's Ruskin speech which unleashed a tide of educational reaction; and, most amazingly from 17 years of Conservative office when, for all their attempts to re-introduce selection by the back door, no minister dared do so openly, in spite of John Major's call for a grammar school in every town. Crosland's legacy is that, without legislation and without any new resources (except for the raising of the school leaving age) he encouraged local education authorities to consolidate comprehensive schooling *as a principle*. He resisted any research into the comprehensive principle: the idea of a research project, he told Maurice Kogan:

> implied that research can tell you what your objectives ought to be. But it can't. Our belief in comprehensive reorganisation was a product of fundamental value judgements about equity and equal opportunity and social division as well as about education. Research can help you achieve your objectives... but it can't tell you whether you should go comprehensive or not – that's a basic value judgement.

Founded on the rock of a Crosland value judgement, the abolition of selection at the age of 11 became politically irreversible.

He was always conscious, however, that inner-city and suburban comprehensives were, and probably always would be, very different animals. Urged on by 'Chelly' Halsey, his sociology mentor, he tried to mitigate the educational disadvantage of inner-city schools with a policy of educational priority areas. In 1967, he injected £16million to improve the buildings of these schools; this was later extended to give the teachers in them a salary premium. He never believed this policy would have dramatic results; but he rightly saw it a raising the morale of the teachers within them.

If the bloom faded on the comprehensive idea in the 1970s and 1980s it was probably because of a curricular and a training deficit. Far too little attention was paid to what children should learn in these schools; as a result, in many of them, an academic curricular diet was imposed on thousands of young people for whom it was simply not appropriate; and, as mergers between grammar and secondary modern schools took place, grammar school teachers were put in charge of classes where many found very difficult to cope. This problem was exacerbated by a crisis in teacher supply; the postwar 'baby boomers' were flooding into the secondary schools; all sort of stratagems were devised to train more teachers – new colleges were opened and existing ones doubled in size. All this tended to suck the best teachers from the schools into the training colleges which were hard put to it to keep going, never mind prepare student teachers for a wholly new secondary school system. If faith in the secondary school declined over the next two decades, this had less to do with comprehensive schools and the democratisation of the system than with the problems of teacher supply which postwar demographic turbulence was producing.

Nor could Crosland, as minister, impact much on the curriculum. The curricula of both the schools and the teacher training colleges were still 'no-go' areas for ministers in the mid-1960s, jealously guarded as the exclusive responsibility of the teachers – while in reality the secondary school curriculum was almost wholly entirely a function of universities' entrance requirements.

Ideally, the comprehensive revolution should have been a project which involved matching new teaching skills to a new curriculum within a new educational philosophy. Some comprehensives schools recognised this and tried to do something about it; and one or two – like Countesthorpe in Leicestershire – were almost broken in the process. But Crosland was right to start with the school structure, even if the absence of a similar driving force within local authorities and the teaching profession to tackle training and the curriculum made many comprehensive schools pale and unsatisfactory shadows of the grammar schools they had replaced; nor did the universities help. Apart from a few Oxford and Cambridge colleges, worried that they might be losing out of working-class talent, the comprehensive revolution passed the universities by; they did nothing to adapt their entrance procedures to the new situation.

THE PUBLIC SCHOOLS

Crosland's other 'failure' was with the public schools, but it was not for want of trying. He had identified them 5 years earlier in *The Conservative Enemy* as the fount of Britain's social problems:

> This privileged stratum of education is the exclusive preserve of the wealthier classes, socially and physically segregated from the state educational system, it is the greatest single cause of stratification and class consciousness in Britain.

Labour policy had always been a vague one of 'integrating' the public schools, a policy which was tried by Butler in 1944 – and which failed. Once the abolition of selection was established as part of Labour policy, integration became patently impossible. These were highly selective schools and it was absurd to pretend otherwise. So Labour policy in 1964 was a cop out – a Commission to suggest ways of dealing with these schools.

In the event, Crosland's Public Schools Commission was a non-starter. The comprehensive project concerned schools over which the government had some control; over the public schools it had none. The Commission's terms of reference were written not to apply to the public schools as such but rather the fact that they were *boarding* schools. A majority of the Commission invented an impractical scheme to seduce a few of the schools into taking 50 per cent of their pupils with fees paid by local authorities as a first step to being integrated into the state sector, with a Boarding School Commission to make it all happen. It was a tortuous compromise which never would have come off. John Davies (of the CBI), Tom Howarth (of St Paul's) and Kitty Anderson (of North London Collegiate) turned the scheme down firmly and politely; John Vaizey was less polite: a close friend of Crosland's (who sent his own son to Eton after a chat with the High Master on the occasion of the Commission visit to the school) he rubbished the whole idea:

> The main objection to private schools is that they are socially divisive. Some of them happen to have beds. It therefore seems less revolutionary to change the bodies in the beds than to eliminate the beds. It is as though Henry VIII had not dismantled the monasteries but filled them with social need cases, after an exhaustive social survey of the number of people in the population who felt the urge for a life of contemplation in a cell. There is a degree of confusion in attempting to 'solve' a social question by throwing out the middle class and replacing it by a different social group.[2]

In speaking later to Maurice Kogan, Crosland bore out his wife's impression that he had become 'not very interested in the public schools'. He played down the Commission as simply checking out 'whether a compromise was possible. They certainly produced a detailed scheme', he said, 'but unfortunately nobody much liked it'. The passionate social revolutionary had been cooled and tempered by the reality of ministerial office. He quickly realised that private education was too tough a nut for Wilson's reformist administration to tackle.

OPENING UP HIGHER EDUCATION: THE POLYTECHNICS

Crosland detested elitism; he also disliked, perhaps more in retrospect, his time in the senior common room of Trinity College, Oxford. Beyond that, however, he did not come to the ministry with strong views about the future shape of higher education. In the normal course of events, the Robbins Report – which had been accepted by Edward Boyle under the Conservatives – would have been gradually implemented cloning, as it did, sub-Oxbridge residential campuses on to the fringes of England's cathedral cities; but when he arrived at the DES he was deluged with advice not to do so. The reaction against Robbins had begun. Eric Robinson the former President of the Association of Teachers in Technical Institutions and Tyrrell Burgess, an LSE academic and a prolific journalist on the subject, lobbied him to develop a wholly different form of post-school education, based on the various local authority colleges in the 'further education' sector. His deputy secretary in charge of this area, Toby Weaver, was also passionate for a pluralist system and a higher education sector which would both attract students who wanted to put knowledge and skills together; Weaver wrote a speech for Crosland to deliver at Woolwich Polytechnic in the summer of 1965, describing the plan as a 'binary policy'. Crosland liked the Robinson–Burgess–Weaver line but, as he put it to Maurice Kogan, he had not digested the arguments and he jumped the gun:

> I began by making an appalling blunder, from which I learnt a lesson I shall never forget... I said to the press when I first went to the DES that I wouldn't make any pronouncements on major policy for the first six months and I broke the rule by making the Woolwich speech... I then had only a superficial knowledge of the subject and every change I made in the draft of the speech made it worse. Incredible. It came out in a manner calculated to infuriate almost everybody you can think of and in public relations terms it did considerable harm to the policy. But the more I thought about it subsequently, the more I became utterly convinced that the policy was right.

Once again, because Crosland relied on his basic instincts, he did the right thing. In spite of a bitter row in the Labour Party (fuelled by university teachers who, quite wrongly, saw the binary divide as a sort of 18+) he produced a White Paper the following year proposing 30 polytechnics, which, 20 years later, became the vehicle of expanding the participation rate in higher education from 10 per cent to 30 per cent.

The Crosland instinct once again was proved right; his 'binary' polytechnic policy provided an alternative model of what 'peoples' universities' could be like; little by little, they were copied by more orthodox universities and enabled expansion to take place. The polytechnics did quite as much to open up education to the disadvantaged as the abolition of the 11 +.

A BEACON OF THE 1960s

It has become fashionable to decry the 'permissive' 1960s as the decade when everything went wrong with Britain. Abortion, divorce, comprehensive schools and the student revolt are often linked as examples of degeneration and decline. I have always seen the decade as a highly creative one in which Britain began the process of renewing its institutions. In any event, it was certainly a decade of egalitarian sentiment. Crosland's fundamental achievement at education was his ability to recognise a trend and go with the egalitarian tide. He saw education as the powerhouse of Labour's social policies because he had spent the previous decade stimulating change and writing about it and because his American wife took every opportunity to remind him what a class-ridden place Britain still was. In social terms, at the DES, he was the man for the hour.

But he was no socialist dreamer. He was a hard-headed economist as well as an egalitarian. The most pejorative adjective in the *Future of Socialism* is 'chiliastic' – that naive insistence on millennial perfection which had plagued Labour policies in the past. He remained throughout the 1960s a passionate Keynesian and still believed that equality would come though growth. Above all, for all his reputation for frivolity and wit, he was a complete and ambitious politician, who wanted a key role in Labour's destiny. Another recollection:

> Earlier, in the hot late summer of 1966, Harold Wilson's government, in spite of its enormous majority, was in a mess, desperately trying to prop up an overvalued pound with emergency legislation on prices and incomes. It became the first of a number of seasons of anti-Wilson plot rumours. All sorts of stories were circulating about replacing him and a whole range of aspirant prime ministers, discreetly through their Parliamentary Private Secretaries, let it be known that they were interested. The August silly season speculative press

became absurd – Jenkins for PM, Callaghan for PM, even Crossman for PM. They were all doing it. At one point, in exasperation, Tony said to me: 'Why the fuck don't I ever read about Crosland for PM; what the hell are you doing about it?' I would not have known where to start; nor, however much I admired his style as minister of education, had it ever occurred to me that he was a plausible prime minister.

It later dawned on me that, just as he seemed to be totally concentrating on his education brief, his mind was also on his own next step and the chances of preferment within the process. But in 1967, his colleagues did not rate him. Dick Crossman, in his diaries, describes Crosland in Cabinet (a judgement he later modifies) as 'curiously lightweight'.

Because he was so exacting intellectually, he remained an ambiguous figure to many others in the PLP. One needed very high standards to be admitted to his charmed circle of acolytes, a position to which, as his *education* PPS, I never fully graduated. But I was allowed a glimpse through the curtains at Crosland, the potential PM:

> I once, in a moment of naive foolishness, asked who Bernstein was. To Tony, only political and economic illiterates did not know the great German revisionist–Marxist on whom he, Tony, had justified his whole career in politics and whose ideas formed a central theme of his great book, *The Future of Socialism*, which I had only inadequately read. From that moment, I was beyond the political pale. But I was allowed as PPS to convene a weekly seminar with his authentic revisionist fan club, the embryo social democratic party, consisting of the three new generation MPs, David Marquand, David Owen and John Mackintosh, whom Tony felt were sufficiently witty, politically literate and ideologically reliable to

have the privilege of discussing the current state of the nation with him on a regular basis. My role was to pour the whisky and listen, as a candidate member of the Labour Right – who might one day be admitted to the secret garden but whose opinions on the central issues of politics and economics were, for the moment, not yet mature enough to be heard.

This ability to concentrate equally and deeply on both politics and education was an enormous strength. It kept his political feet on the ground and it gave him a stature among his colleagues both in Cabinet and in the Party which few other ministers achieved. Soon after he left Education, Wilson devalued the pound and Callaghan, the Chancellor, resigned; in the crucial Commons debate, the task of stating the case for devaluation (and therefore for economic growth) was given to Crosland; 10 years later when the IMF were enforcing deflation on another Labour government, it was left to Crosland put the anti-IMF case in Cabinet. The Parliamentary Party never rated him; somehow he never threw off his old playboy image. But he rated himself as a politician and his self confidence made him a better Education Minister.

None of his Labour successors began to match him in terms of either achievement or style. Patrick Gordon Walker was a tired disaster in the job, Ted Short was competent but pedestrian; Reg Prentice was already intent on breaking up the Labour Party, his mind never fully on the job; Fred Mulley (to whom I also acted a PPS) was competent but hopelessly uncharismatic; and Shirley Williams proved too much of a ditherer as the Callaghan government stumbled towards the abyss. If David Blunkett wants a role model in his present job, he should study the Crosland tenure of ministerial office at the Department of Education and Science.

Notes

1. Circular 10/65; see discussion on pp. 61–2.
2. Public Schools Commission, 1st Report, Vol. 1 (HMSO, 1968), Note of Reservation by John Vaizey, p. 221.

8 Environment Secretary*
Humphrey Cole

Except for a single casual encounter I did not meet Crosland until he became Secretary of State for the Environment. But I should have done. I had joined the Department of Economic Affairs (DEA) soon after he left for Education. When the DEA was abolished Crosland became Secretary of State for Local Government and Regional Planning with a kind of overview, but only a shadowy power, over two of the Departments – Ministry of Housing and Local Government (MHLG) and Ministry of Transport (MOT) – that were later to form the DOE. He laid claim to my services as the senior economist in government service working on regional issues. But so did Benn, and to my sorrow Crosland lost the argument. Fairly soon I had had enough of the Ministry of Technology (Mintech) and I switched to the DOE on the day it was formed. By the time, three and half years later, that Crosland arrived at the DOE I was rather pretentiously known as its Director-General of Economics and Resources.

I find it hard to feel myself back in those days of political crisis of February and March 1974. The crisis was of a different order to the simple crisis that had confronted the earlier Wilson Government in November 1964. Then Crosland had been annoyed to arrive at the new DEA to find that the key economic decision – not to devalue – had been taken before he even got there. But, although the Labour majority then was tiny, the election had not been so

---
* Written for this volume.

fraught as it was to be in 1974. Heath had called the latter on the issue 'Who governs – the Government or the striking miners?' – and the electorate returned an unclear answer in the form of a hung Parliament. I remember talking with a colleague during the election and speculating about the likely role of the Civil Service if the result was to be a hung Parliament. With the divide between the main parties so bitter – with lawless noises emanating from both extremes of the political spectrum – I guessed it would mean a stronger role for the civil service.

How wrong can one be – and especially so about the DOE. I did not personally see much of Crosland in action in those first few weeks. But all of us learned quickly enough there was to be none of that – he was in complete charge, he knew what he wanted done, and what he asked from his officials was the administrative drive and ingenuity to get them done.

He made no secret of his pleasure and surprise at the quality of the support he got from the Department – much better than he had experienced in any of his other ministerial jobs. He retained his affection and respect for it to the end of his time there – especially for his private office. Achieving that kind of rapport is vital for an incoming Minister. But very few can arrive feeling that the Department was their own creation. In his last ministerial post he had planned the merger. Now – with no bones about who was in charge *vis-à-vis* his other ministers – he had the chance to make a success of his own creation. He had direct access to any civil servant he chose, not only through another minister. He particularly relished his right to decide what was important and/ or interesting enough for him to deal with personally and the chance to leave to other ministers what was boring. Alas for him, some subjects are both important and boring, especially the annual haggle with the Treasury and colleagues about public expenditure plans that was called PESC. He said he hated it and meant it! And not just because his economics said to him that the economy could be run at a higher level of demand than the Treasury thought wise. It was also not the way he liked thinking through his priorities. He preferred to tackle subjects one at a time. But that did not mean that he did not take it seriously – once describing it as the most important thing a minister does. Nor could he wholly escape large boring meetings which were a characteristic component item of official life in those days!

Crosland was well prepared to deal with the policy issues of his new Department. He had held the shadow DOE portfolio in opposition, and had used the opportunity to re-think through his objectives and their relation to policy. His position away from the centre of the party rows about Europe and industrial policy had helped him in this, though not in other ways. By and large the manifesto, at least as far as it concerned the DOE's responsibilities, reflected the results of his own thinking. Given his intellectual standing and his genuine expertise in the area, no DOE official was going lightly to challenge his demands on the grounds that they did not make sense. They value their perception of their role as executants of their Minister's wants – but much more so when it is clear and intellectually coherent – and especially when it was in the manifesto!

These were, of course, the days of long manifestos with numerous commitments – and also of deep suspicion in Labour left-wingers about the dangers of office undermining worthy socialist proposals. Mostly what got done in those early days can be included under the head of implementing the manifesto. As manifestos have now become less comprehensive it is more relevant today to write about the things that do not come under that head. I would merely note in passing that he did not slavishly enact what was in the manifesto. The dubious proposal to control commercial rents was, after a while, dropped. He also had doubts about the wisdom of controlling private furnished rents, but felt the political commitment was too firm to draw back.

One particularly tricky early decision he had to take concerned the rate support grant (RSG), where an order prepared by the Tories was waiting for submission to Parliament. Inflation, rating revaluation and local government reorganisation had combined to make this subject a political minefield. Whatever was done there would be large losers (as well as winners) among householders who received no corresponding gains in better services. But he wrestled this one out as a clear issue of socialist principles and insisted on amending the order. 'Now clear: redistribution of RSG morally and socially right but politically definitely wrong. Good and socialist policies not electorally popular', he noted. What is interesting about this reflection is not that the left of the party thought he was wrong. It is as interesting that he does not consider whether the last-minute switching of expected grant levels is wise in the context of the relations between central and local government and of local fiscal responsibility. Choosing the formula for the rate support grant after close examination of the political consequences of alternative parameters became a regular feature of the annual settlement under successive governments. It has probably been an important factor in undermining local fiscal responsibility.

A little later he responded to Mrs Thatcher's call to abolish local rates by setting up the Layfield Committee to examine local government finance. This was primarily a political move, since he felt that there was no realistic alternative to the rates and expected Layfield to say so. How he would have reacted to their eventual call for much more of local authorities' revenue to be raised locally if local democracy were to flourish one cannot be sure. But I doubt he would have been persuaded to take the issue seriously, especially as they chose a local income tax as the recommended means. Given the high level of income tax at the time, that was virtually a non-starter. But it was a missed opportunity in the continuing saga of semi-intentional downgrading of local independence characteristic of all governments at that time.

Crosland's other innovation in this field – the beefing up of the consultative machinery with local government – was much more successful. He thus helped greatly to improve relations and understanding between central and local government when they might easily have got worse. His adoption of the simple but effective 'The party's over' to get the message of economy over worked wonders, even though it was not a message he welcomed having to give.

The government had by now won its thin but working majority in Parliament; but it had not yet got the economy under control. As 1975 unrolled the issue of the total level of public expenditure became acute. In Crosland's considered assessment of the record of the 1964 Labour government he had acclaimed the rise in the share of public expenditure from 41 to 48 per cent of GNP as evidence of its socialist success. Public expenditure was to be preferred to private expenditure because the social wage was the way to help the needy of society. So the cuts which were being sought by the Treasury were in danger of becoming an assault on the core of his socialism. He was sceptical whether deflation on that scale was needed. So his inclination was to resist to the utmost the cuts that were being sought in his programmes. But he was grudgingly becoming more uncomfortable about the level income tax rates had reached. He was ready intellectually to acknowledge that the level of tax on high earned incomes might be counter-productive because of its effects on incentives and tax avoidance. But it was the plight at the other end – the poverty trap – that hit him emotionally. High marginal tax rates on the working poor was not his idea of socialist priorities.

This conflict surfaced in his decision to fight uncompromisingly for his housing expenditure, where he forbade his officials even to discuss possible cuts with the Treasury. Promoting council housing was so clearly an issue of social equity. But he let us try to find a compromise in the other fields. He took the housing issues direct to his Cabinet colleagues – with some success – and had no doubt that he had been right to do so. But he retained a lingering suspicion that he should have done the same thing across the board. By the time the next round of PESC came along he had left for the Foreign Office. His continuing fight for less deflation at the time of the IMF loan is well known.

During 1975 Wilson began to make more use in inter-departmental business of Crosland's standing as an economist – first in industrial policy and then in the transformation of the social contract into a more effective prices and incomes policy. He was very pleased at this recognition. Fortunately for the Department this was not for him a demanding call upon his time – nor did he need much advice from me. It did not interfere with his determination to embark on two very ambitious across-the-board reviews of policy – one of transport and the other of housing.

The first was virtually completed in his time at the DOE – the Orange consultative paper 'Transport Policy' was actually published in the week after he became Foreign Secretary. The full housing review was started later – it had begun as a narrow review of housing finance – and was not published until 1977. In both cases the bulk of the work was done in-house, but there was more consultation with outside experts in housing. Both were firmly led by Crosland himself and not by the supporting minister in charge of that subject area, whose role was fairly minor. For transport the official support was organised from the Department's central policy unit under my charge, and so I was actively engaged in its conduct. For housing a special unit was set up – so perhaps my most important contribution was to switch many economists to the back-up analytic team from other areas of the Department. I shall say more about the former, even though the latter was much nearer to Crosland's heart

Fortunately, officials had recently completed an internal review of transport policy for the previous government; so we were reasonably up to date in terms of data analysis and identification of policy issues. As important was the review of transport policy Crosland had organised under the auspices of *Socialist Commentary*, a revisionist Labour journal, while in opposition. That had been much better researched and funded than oppositions can normally afford. So we should have got off to a flying start.

Crosland chose not to give us much personal guidance at that stage. It might have been better if he had – at least in principle. But, if you press for guidance when someone is not ready to concentrate enough to give considered answers, one may regret having done so. Not all his less considered remarks were helpful, even though they did reflect genuine feelings. Their timing escapes me, but among transport comments I remember. 'Road maintenance – why not more use of those valuable French notices *chaussée déformée*, instead of wasting money on too good road surfaces' – at a time when the problem of heavy lorries breaking up under-designed roads was becoming serious. Or again. 'New roads should be built only when congestion on the existing roads shows that they are genuinely needed' – a kind of Bangkok–Teheran solution at a time when planning, designing and building a new road was taking up to

15 years. Or again 'There is far too much spare capacity on both trunk roads and British Rail' - the reaction to a week-end visit, I think to Birmingham, but it may have been to Banbury, his weekend cottage, there by road and back by rail. Such remarks do indicate instinctive priorities – in this case a distrust often well founded (cf. Maplin[1]) of expenditure claims pressed by 'experts'. But with Crosland in particular, one learned to wait until he was ready to give undivided attention to your problems.

Even so it was disappointing that, when the review was submitted to Crosland, he found that it did not fully match up to what he wanted. I think there were two reasons for this. First he felt some of it did not come up to his own high intellectual standards – which of course it did not! So he wanted to go through it carefully himself to check how far the reasoning would stand up to his, and then the public's, scrutiny. Second, was it in content a clearly socialist policy – in his sense of the term? We knew he would not have an 'integrated transport policy'. Indeed, he told us not to use that term, for he felt the phrase enshrined too well what he disliked about much instinctive Labour thinking on transport – the command approach that had little time for user choice and often pushed sectional interests in the name of planning. But did it have enough about social costs – not just the externalities such as congestion costs which figure so importantly in any transport analysis, but also the social duty to look after the transport needs of the poor and the deprived?

To be honest, he did not say quite this at the time. I have surmised some of it from later remarks of his to me. But he used the report as the basis for the next stage, in which he decided to do the rest himself with the help of just one official (not me). For the time it took he concentrated on that task to the exclusion of other work. It paid off.

When he had finished he was justifiably proud of his new genre of policy consultative document and insisted that it should not be printed as a conventional Green Paper but as a new Orange Paper to serve as a model for all to follow. Sadly it was not printed in time for him to launch his *magnum opus* on the public himself, for the timing of Wilson's resignation was such that he missed that by three days.

And so to housing – the more ambitious review of the two. *Prima facie* there was a very strong case for a comprehensive review. High inflation and high interest rates were playing merry hell with the relative prices between sectors, thus changing unpredictably the real values of incomes net of housing costs in the owner-occupied and rented sectors. That raised issues critical to Crosland's concept of socialism. And with owner-occupation fast spreading down the social scale the image of it as a tenure for the 'better off' was becoming less and less tenable – and not just for electoral reasons. So it was important for the financial relativities of the main sectors to be studied in depth, and new structures of support devised that would restore stability between the sectors and protect the worst off. But the work had to be done in the context of the changing real needs for housing. Except in London, the crude shortage of housing had been largely eliminated; but more houses were still needed to cope with the falling average household size – especially the growth of elderly single-person households with their special needs. Nothing seemed likely to stem the continuing decline of the private rented sector, but its role in the inner cities was still vital. Finally rehabilitation of the older stock could take a higher priority than before. So support had to be more selective than heretofore, yet still stable enough to give confidence to the builders and planners.

Historically, the Ministry of Housing and Local Government had been weak on analysis and on data collection – especially in contrast with the Ministry of Transport since Barbara Castle's day. Within the unified DOE matters had been improving, but the contrast persisted. So there was less of a flying start with this review than for the transport one. On the other hand, Crosland cared much more about this area of policy. Hence he gave more time and effort to the initial stages, and was willing to involve more outsiders – even at the risk of some boredom.

Certainly he was well pleased at the way the work was shaping up at the last overview meeting I can remember attending. At that stage, it had become clear that the policy proposals would be numerous but not radical Whether he would have remained content with that in the later stages if he had still been at the Department one cannot say. I think he would have been proud of the thoroughness and quality of the analysis. But I suspect that, as in transport, he would have wanted to make a concentrated personal effort to improve both the policy and the presentation before publication – with what results who can say? But at that late stage he would have found it hard to transform the conclusions.

Was this sort of result inevitable from the start of the review? One academic participant in the review thought not and wrote:

> The shortcoming is not that the proposals emerging from the review were modest but that they were wrongly conceived. Instead of attempting to develop policy changes appropriate to the current and developing situations, appeasement of the largest number of relevant interests became the overriding consideration.

A savage charge indeed and not one plausible in relation to Crosland, unless any attention to electoral considerations is out of bounds for a practising politician. But the same critic also wrote:

Thus one comes sadly to the conclusion that there is little alternative to something like the package of limited proposals.... of the 1975–7 Housing Policy Review.[2]

I suspect that Crosland would himself have had sympathy with this sadness. When he started both reviews he had expectations of achieving more in terms of policy proposals than he eventually did. This goes back to the strength of his egalitarian principles. Although a revisionist in terms of 'Clause four socialism' he was so radical in terms of his hatred for class-based inequalities that he had to search for a package of policies that would make a radical impact on these (cf. comprehensive schools). A *sotto voce* theme of both reviews was that he did not find them. In transport this was not a major disappointment, and what was in the Orange Paper was subsequently implemented by his successor. But his aim of favouring the bus industry as *par excellence* the mode of the less well off was largely frustrated by the remorseless spread of car ownership at all social levels. In housing, much of the limited package of reforms was also implemented. The flexible financial framework, which was designed to facilitate the implementation of selective local housing policies favourable to the public sector, later proved no obstacle to the Conservatives' very different aims. He would have hated what did happen under them, but it is hard to see what he could have done to prevent that. Even if he had been more willing to be ruthless about reducing general subsidy all round (as all experts tend to favour), would it have made all that difference? The chequered history of inner-city policy gives ground for scepticism.

However Crosland would have found it hard to set up either review on the basis that he should not be genuinely radical – still less that his egalitarian principles were flawed – which would have been the implication of accepting a limited agenda from the start. Should one accept the limitation that policy reforms should be focused on identifying alternative marginal changes and the objectives they should serve? Such reforms would then have a greater chance of surviving the next election! But I would draw a rather different lesson. Given that it normally makes sense to be realistically unambitious about the aims of any piece of policy review, one needs a rather different approach to the process of such review when it has been decided that something genuinely radical is required. The critical period is likely to be the initial stage, when the parameters of the review are being set. Active political participation at that stage is essential not just in defining wish lists but in facing up to the key problems that make the achievement of those wishes problematical. Crosland probably put too much of his effort in at the end when the scope for radical thinking had become circumscribed by the work already done. But it is also plausible that more initial work by him – or by politically minded persons able to think radically like him – would have shown that neither housing nor transport were really ripe for radical review. But in saying this now I am indulging in the luxury of hindsight – I was wholly pleased at the time with his decisions to undertake both reviews.

Notes

1. A proposal for a third London airport near Foulness, on the Essex coast. See p. 140.
2. J. B. Cullingworth, *Essays on Housing Policy*, (London: Allen & Unwin, 1979).

9 Foreign Secretary*
Michael Palliser

Tony Crosland had barely 10 months in office as Foreign and Commonwealth Secretary, before being struck down at the height of his intellectual powers. That was a desperately short time for any considered judgement of his quality in the post; and it was an open secret that for him – as has subsequently been true of others – the Foreign Office was not the department that he really coveted. But if the Treasury was not to be his, then at least the Foreign Office represented the kind of political and intellectual challenge that he always relished; and he had for years taken a well informed interest in international affairs and especially in international democratic socialism.

So he brought to his office an instinctive and intelligent awareness of the world and its problems. This was a useful background to the decisions and judgements he had to make. But he was almost too aware of his basic inexperience of the important detail that needed to be understood in dealing with the multifarious issues that daily crowd the desk of a Foreign Secretary. In foreign affairs, however important the issues, the devil is constantly in the detail; and Tony Crosland was ever reluctant to reach a decision until he had mastered the detail. This often meant for him several hours – sometimes days – of careful reading, study and discussion with his advisers before he took a decision; whereas the need for a decision often seemed to them too urgent for that process.

This meant, inevitably, that to some of his officials he seemed overly cautious and a shade dilettante. This too superficial impression was enhanced by his

---
* Written for this volume.

own very evident irritation with the inescapable burdens of his daily round; the need to see foreign Ambassadors and visiting dignitaries, to attend constant meetings in London and abroad, to be briefed for them all; and thereby, as he saw it, to waste so much of the time he needed for the more important task of rigorously studying the political issues that confronted him before he had to reach decisions on them. But to those of us who saw him frequently – and his very need for help and advice meant that a few of us did indeed see much of him – he came across as a very different person. He was essentially reflective; and, in the words I used about him in a short addition to the obituary notice in *The Times*:

> we came greatly to respect his handling of public business – his subtle perception, his penetrating insight, his concentration on the essential, his accuracy of mind, his intolerance of the slipshod, his economy of words and his sometimes abrupt but consistently effective chairmanship.'

Of course, those very qualities meant that he was not always easy to approach, and if he was worried or anxious about something – usually because he had not had time enough to reflect thoroughly about it – he could be brusque and apparently off-hand. But as the weeks went by and he became more familiar both with the subjects and with the speed and efficiency with which they were handled in the office, I think he came in fact to enjoy the work, which he saw as having 'a compelling intellectual fascination'. In a New Year message to the Diplomatic Service, he acknowledged 'the intellectual qualities, efficiency and sheer good humour' of its members. The message was no doubt drafted for his signature; but significantly the qualities he praised were indeed those that he himself most appreciated.

What did he achieve in those few months at the end of his life? It is always difficult to ascribe success (or failure) to a Foreign Secretary, because foreign policy is essentially a continuum. There is a tendency for one man (we have not yet had a woman Foreign Secretary) to start something and for it to be carried forward, not always to a conclusion, by his successor, whether of the same or another political party. In Tony Crosland's case this was true of Rhodesia: an excessively difficult problem at the time, to which he devoted great effort and attention, but without making much progress. It formed a significant item on the agenda of his first meeting with the already legendary US Secretary of State, Henry Kissinger.

Kissinger was due to pass briefly through London, on his way back to Washington one weekend, and Crosland had never met him. Kissinger suggested a meeting (he probably had Heathrow in mind!). Crosland was both keen to meet this quintessential professional and yet apprehensive of displaying his own lack of experience. So his instinct was to lie low and use the weekend (when he was due at meetings in his constituency at Grimsby) as an excuse for postponing a meeting to a more auspicious occasion. His determined advisers, political as well as professional, dissented; he really could not fob off the US Secretary of State in that way.

So Crosland suggested an ingenious compromise designed, by transferring the venue for the meeting, slightly to enhance his own standing. Let the meeting be held in his parliamentary constituency of Grimsby, where he had to be that weekend in any case. The RAF station there, with its large airfield, would enable Kissinger to fly there in Air Force One; and they could meet over breakfast at the Officers' Mess! And so it was. Kissinger was undoubtedly taken aback, but also intrigued to meet this audacious man. He kindly gave a lift up to Grimsby in his plane from Heathrow to both the US Ambassador, Ann Armstrong, and to myself. And during the flight he said to me in semi-jocular fashion 'He'll owe me one for this!' But the meeting (over a splendid RAF breakfast) was a success, at least in personal terms. Kissinger was as knowledgeable as ever, without being patronising. Crosland said less and was characteristically cautious. But this was a conversation between two intellectual equals, however different their background and social upbringing. They clearly respected and quite enjoyed each other.

Crosland worked hard at the Rhodesian problem. But he made little headway; and after him David Owen also made valiant efforts, in semi-partnership with the then US Secretary of State, to resolve the issue. But in the end it fell to the next Conservative Foreign Secretary, Lord Carrington, to bring matters to a successful end. I am sure Crosland would have welcomed the Lancaster House Agreement, which was certainly in tune with his own approach.

His political skills – and even more his political courage – were severely tested by the so-called 'cod war' with Iceland. He was MP for Grimsby, one of Britain's leading fishing ports, whose fleet was deeply involved in the imbroglio. To resolve the matter, as Crosland did, quickly, sensibly but also in recognising the greater needs of Iceland over those of the UK, was a brave example of putting the wider national interest over the narrow local one. But it was difficult for him to have to make the choice and then to defend it, in Parliament and in Grimsby. It redounded greatly to his credit.

Tony Crosland was a 'European'; not unconditionally and he sometimes disappointed those more emotionally committed than he. But he believed in the European Community (as it then was) and in British membership, while bringing to it and its problems the same intellectually rigorous analysis as he brought to every problem – and thus inevitably on occasion finding the Community wanting, even if the judgements he reached did not always strike those who knew the Community well as either fair or constructive. But he tackled the task of presiding over Britain's Presidency with vigour and determination and made a considerable impression on his colleagues in the EC Council; an impression enhanced by an excellent keynote speech to the European Parliament.

Crosland's untimely death left so much unfinished, indeed unbegun. By any standards he was a major political figure and, had he lived, he might have come to be seen as a major Foreign Secretary. He was not long enough in the office for that judgement to be made. But it says much for his memory that those of his subordinates in the Foreign Office who saw most of him were also those who came most to respect, admire and feel real affection for him. And no account of him as Foreign Secretary would be complete without a tribute to the huge part played in his life, both personally and in his official functions, by Susan Crosland. She brought humour, intelligence and candid comment to his all too rare moments of leisure; and with the same qualities she brightened all official functions they attended together, and helped to make them a little less burdensome for him. She showed herself to be not only an attractive and powerful personality in her own right, but also the ideal complement to Tony himself. He knew it; it lightened his life, as her presence at his side must also have lightened his dying.

Part III
Continuing Legacy

10 Crosland as Apparatchik*
Brian Brivati

> Look, forget about all this talk about intellectualism. We are apparatchiks.
>
> (Brivati, 1992)

INTRODUCTION

After the death of Hugh Gaitskell the small patience that Tony Crosland had with being an apparatchik was exhausted. But while Gaitskell was alive and the leader of the party, Crosland was prepared to be a chief of staff and get his hands dirty in the low-level business of party factionalism. It was the one period of his career in which he played the role of a political operator, albeit one who managed to combine being an organiser with being a political intellectual. His failure–and, more broadly, the failure of the revisionist wing of the party–to continue to operate in this hands-on, overtly factional way, cost them dear in the long run. The left, never as well organised as the Gaitskellites supposed, though always reasonably efficient, learnt important lessons from the experience of the 1959–64 Parliament. They applied these lessons and did not lose the organisational impetus until the revisionist networks were partially rekindled in the late 1970s in the various prologues to schism. By this time Crosland's sense of loyalty had triumphed over his distaste for the left and, had he lived, he

---

* Written for this volume.

would have been unlikely to have joined the SDP split. But in the earlier phase, harnessed to the chariot of Gaitskell's leadership, he was a willing participant in the most successful piece of internal factionalism the right of the Labour Party ever mustered, the Campaign for Democratic Socialism(CDS).

CROSLAND AND THE ORIGINS OF THE CDS

The story of the founding of the CDS has been told before and is recounted briefly here with an emphasis on Crosland's involvement.[1] By the Spring of 1960 it looked as though Gaitskell and the revisionist wing of the Labour Party faced defeat. Crosland had privately warned against the move on Clause Four on tactical grounds. He now swung into action, uncharacteristically – and slightly infuriating for Gaitskell – lecturing the leader on the need for a fresh approach in a series of memoranda on the general theme: 'Can we do anything to make our leadership-system more professional and less amateur and haphazard?'

Crosland had been a feature of the Gaitskellite networks since the early 1950s when, in his first Parliament as an MP, he had worked hard and conscientiously. He was, for example, one of the people brought together by Gaitskell in 1952 to try and oppose the Bevanites in the House of Commons and Gaitskell praised him for his efforts in his diary for that year. In 1954, when Bill Rodgers and Dick Taverne convened a small debating club, known as the Group, he spoke to them about the need for political work and when *The Future of Socialism* was published 'the great man was wheeled in' to talk to them.[2] They, in common with most of the political world, debated amongst themselves the implications of the book. This activity was an expression of the way in which Crosland became closer to Gaitskell both personally and politically as the decade progressed. Crosland's attitude to this kind of political work fluctuated, but Gaitskell relied on him and others for consistent support and ideas. Though doing the revisionist's tiny equivalent of the rubber chicken circuit, Crosland's role was never predominantly organisational. From 1956, his role was ideological. In this respect his contribution was remarkable. By 1960, the reception of *The Future of Socialism* was such that Stuart Hall devoted a lengthy article to attacking it in the first edition of the *New Left Review*:

> The ideological battles have long since been joined and won. First Gaitskell assented; and then, one after another, the up and coming intellectuals in the leadership... By the time *Industry and Society* appeared at Brighton in 1957 the picture of reformed capitalism, the managerial revolution and applied Keynesian economics which Mr Crosland described had already began to be extended across the face of official policy.[3]

During the spring of 1960, in the aftermath of the defeat at the 1959 general election, Gaitskell's leadership came under sustained attack. His attempt to revise Clause Four, and his stance on nuclear weapons, were being used in a concerted challenge to his position as leader. The left seemed poised to defeat two of the main tenets of the leader's policy making it impossible for him to carry on. The mood of the Gaitskellites was reflected in some rash private talk and personal disillusionment with the Labour Party. Crosland did not discount the possibility of the Party splitting but before doing that advocated organising something to take on the left in the Constituency Labour Parties (CLPs).[4] This was not going to follow the 1952 example of making more speeches in the House of Commons, but was to operate unofficially, through the CLPs and the Trade Union branches.

Crosland's series of letters outlining the need for better organisation had an effect on Gaitskell and he organised a meeting in London between himself, Crosland, Roy Jenkins and Patrick Gordon Walker. The discussion centred on how to deal with the defence question and the Hampstead Set's pessimism was subsequently recounted by Gordon Walker:

> Crosland said that if [Gaitskell] took this line how many would he carry into opposition? He could not hope for 100. [Perhaps 10] said [Gaitskell] who became very angry and rounded on the other 2 sharply and implied that I was a [fudger] of principle. [Crosland] said this would be like the ineffective right-wing breakaway in French party – purely intellectual with supporters like Tomney and Bellenger.[5]

Crosland went from this London meeting to Nuffield to visit his close friend Philip Williams. Williams and Brian Walden told him about their idea for a new grass–roots' centre grouping. His response was 'wildly enthusiastic'[6]. At about the same time Bill Rodgers, who had resigned as general secretary of the Fabian Society in January 1960 and taken a job with the Consumers' Association, arranged a meeting with Tony Crosland at *The Two Chairmen* pub in Dartmouth Street:

> it now seemed to me, in view of the Clause Four dispute, that this was really the time to rally more seriously than ever before people of like minds. I raised with Tony the whole question of liaison on the right in the light of our experience of the Clause Four dispute and of my letter to Hugh Gaitskell.

Rodgers lamented the way that *Tribune* had succeeded in making left-wing policy appeal to young people by giving them a direct input into an organisation and allowing them to meet 'leading *Tribune* figures socially'. This meant that there was 'real cohesion on the left'. Finally he told Crosland what he wanted to see happen: 'Was it possible to get some sort of continuous liaison on the right from Hugh Gaitskell at the top, through Members of the Parliamentary Party, to candidates and key workers in the constituencies?'[7] So Crosland became the link between two small groups of Gaitskellites, one in London and one in Oxford, and the leadership. These three groups were to form the nucleus of CDS.

In further discussions it was decided to assemble a group in London to discuss what should be done. Present at this meeting were representatives from inside and outside the House of Commons. The non-parliamentarians included Dick Taverne, Rodgers' co-organiser of an open letter of support for Gaitskell's leadership published on 3 February 1960 and co-organiser of 1950s' debating society The Group. There was also Ivan Yates, another leading light of The Group, and the author of articles supportive of Gaitskell over Clause 4 in *Reynolds News*, and Michael Shanks, also a Group member, Industrial Editor of the *Financial Times* and author, in 1961, of the revisionist tract *The Stagnant Society*. Shanks, in common with other CDS organisers had spent time in the United States and shared Rodgers' impatience with the lack of organisation on the right of the Labour Party. From the Commons came the four leading members of the Hampstead Set. Rodgers assessed their contributions later:

> Douglas Jay, although always willing to help, didn't play a leading part. Roy Jenkins kept in continuous contact, was always very willing to help and served on Committees, but he was perhaps less close to us in the crucial months than some others.[8]

The two key figures were Patrick Gordon Walker and Tony Crosland. Gordon Walker was supportive and kept Gaitskell informed of what was happening in the CDS and in the liaison committee set up with the trade unions on the selection of parliamentary candidates.[9] But it was Crosland who got the most deeply involved in the early phase of the CDS.

Crosland was clear from the outset that an organisation that was based on Labour Party members and was designed to rally moderate opinion behind the cause of multilateralism, revisionism and Gaitskell's leadership was both necessary and would be well supported. He told Walden that money would not be an object and even that if things went wrong then: 'He did not discount the possibility that eventually the Labour Party would split, and then the role of the New Group would change.'

There was a general consensus amongst the CDS organisers, from Rodgers and Taverne down, that Crosland was the ideological inspiration for the CDS and it is clear from the record that in the early days he played a significant organisational role. The ideological role was made plain by Walden when he wrote the first outline plan for the CDS in May 1960:

> The only policy the group will have is this... an acceptance of modern political, social and economic realities as exemplified in the writings of Crosland and Galbraith.

Rodgers reflected later on Crosland's effect on the early part of the CDS:

> Throughout the period of preparation before the launching of the Campaign Tony Crosland's role was crucial. Not only did he give the intellectual lead reflected in the Manifesto: he also showed a single-mindedness of purpose and discipline which most of us had previously believed he had not possessed. It was he who kept us at it when we

met, mainly at his flat, refusing, for example, to let us have a drink until we had done three hours solid work. He had the authority to keep us together and although he in no way dominated the group he gave it a lead without which much less would have been done.[10]

Dick Taverne, also involved from the outset, shared Rodgers' feelings about Crosland,

> The person who I think contributed most after Bill [Rodgers] was Tony Crosland. At the meetings we went to he was the driving force. He would constantly say 'Look, forget about all this talk about intellectualism. We are apparatchiks.[11]

Walden caught Crosland's mood at the time in a letter to Frank Pickstock:

> Crosland said tonight that he had not felt so happy for years. He believes passionately that all this can be done. Given the initial surge, he believes that the response will astound us all. He made mention of his own personal sense of loneliness until recently – just the thing you and I had discussed.[12]

THE CDS MANIFESTO

Once the groups had met, elected a steering committee and decided on their basic strategy for launching – they would draft a manifesto – Crosland again played a central role. The Manifesto, which was to consist of approximately 600 words and say what they meant by socialism, was to be prepared by the Oxford group and Crosland. Throughout July 1960 the Manifesto was posted between Oxford and London. Crosland had pulled the two groups together, kept them at the job during long meetings and now took the lead in drafting. The first draft that had been written by

Frank Pickstock, an Oxford city councillor and the Campaign's grass-roots' front man, was rather bleak. In part it read:

> Many members of the Labour Party are dismayed that the broad purposes of the Party are being frustrated by the ceaseless activities of sects and pressure groups and feel the need for unity amongst those people, many of whom have given lifelong service to the movement, and who, whilst adhering to the central tradition of the British Labour Movement, recognise that its outlook and policies must be adapted to the economic, social realities of the present day.
>
> Such members are today finding it increasingly impossible to continue active work in the Party when minority groups, unrepresentative of the membership as a whole, use pressure group tactics to impose their will on the Party. The aim of the ... is to form a platform on which the mass of the loyal members of the Labour Party may unite and act together to enable the Party to present to the nation a consistent and responsible policy in conformity with present day needs.

This draft was commented on by Walden, Williams and Pickstock and revised at a further meeting on Sunday 29 May. After this meeting Crosland was invited to rewrite the Manifesto: 'you seemed the obvious person to draft it! (to us anyway)'[13] The Manifesto went through an almost complete change before being presented to a meeting of the steering committee on 26 June, 1960. The main subsequent stages in its evolution were its presentation at meetings in July, August and September, finally it was changed after the Scarborough vote itself when Gaitskell made his famous 'Fight, and Fight and Fight Again speech'. To illustrate the way the drafting evolved, and Crosland's major contribution to it, we can take what came to be the 'ideological background paragraph.'

This began as simply a call for action which was directed at specific targets and open about the form of reorganisation required. Key phrases are shown in *italics*:

> We realise that we ourselves will be charged with being yet another sect. We are forced to act in this way unless we are content to let *the central tradition of the Party* to be destroyed by the doctrinaire, *ideological Marxist doctrines* which are being preached ceaselessly. We call upon *Labour Party loyalists* everywhere to join us in this effort, and to form groups in all local Labour organisations. The purpose of such groups will be to unite active and like-minded people and enable them to act together against the *irresponsible and disruptive activities of doctrinaire groups*, many of them containing ex-members of the Communist Party whose *Marxist–Leninist fervour remains undimmed*. The members of the ... regard it as of the highest importance that the responsible leadership of the Party, namely, the Parliamentary Party, shall receive the support they need from the Party. We cannot expect the electorate to support the Party, when the Party itself gives its *leaders so little loyalty* as it does at the present time.[14]

The specific request that groups form in 'all local Labour organisations' was toned down as the drafting developed. The ideological background paragraph developed drastically and is in recognisable form by the fourth draft which predates the 27 June meeting in London:[15]

> By *central tradition of the Party we mean a non-dogmatic practical socialism*. Though the Labour Party has included many Marxists, its inspiration has been

mainly drawn from trade union, *nonconformist, Christian socialist and radical sources.* The narrow definition of socialism which is prevalent today is making it more and more difficult for many people to ally themselves with the Party.[16]

After three further revisions by the Williams, Crosland and Pickstock team it was presented to the July meeting of the Steering Committee in an almost identical form to the paragraph as finally printed:

> By the *central tradition of the Party we mean a nondoctrinal, practical, humanitarian socialism* – a creed of 'conscience and reform' rather than of class hatred. The British Labour Movement owes its inspiration to British *radicals, trade unionists, nonconformists and Christian Socialists, not to Marx and Lenin.* We oppose the narrow *Marxist definition of socialism which is being insinuated as orthodox Party doctrine,* not only because it repels a growing number of Labour sympathisers but, above all, because it distorts the Party's *ethical, reformist heritage.*[17]

From there originally being numerous references to Marx or Marxism, these are the only ones that remained in the Manifesto as published. During the drafting process Pickstock tended to play a moderating role on Williams' and Crosland's overtly antileftwing paragraphs. For example, Crosland's response to Pickstock's fourth draft, the first to be seen outside Oxford, contained the following paragraph which was quickly deleted:

> We are appalled by the personal venom, directed especially against the Party's elected leaders, shown by some 'socialists' who have forgotten the meaning of the word fraternity. A Party of snarling factions will neither win, nor deserve, the confidence of the electorate.[18]

However Pickstock's role should not be overstated, from his first draft almost nothing remained by the time of publication. Crosland's re-drafts formed the basis of the bulk of the Manifesto as published. Full meetings also contributed to the drafting of the Manifesto. At the meeting on 29 July for instance, Austen Albu, Michael Shanks, Douglas Jay, Tony Dumont, Ivan Yates, Ron Owen, Alec Grant, Dick Taverne, Roy Jenkins, Julius Gould and Oleg Kerensky all recommended amendments, ranging from Dumont's 'less bromide' and Owen's 'Needs more punch' to Albu's 'world government is waffle". During the drafting of the Manifesto one of the members of the group, Niall Macdermott,[19] dropped out because he objected to the Croslandite phrase in paragraph 10 of the pre-Scarborough draft that read: 'we see the nationalisation of all the means of production, distribution and exchange as a dogma irrelevant to our real problems.' The sentence was dropped on the recommendation of Philip Williams so that the section on public ownership read:

> Recognising that public and cooperative and private enterprise all have a part to play in the economy, we regard the public ownership of particular industries or services as a useful technique to be justified on its merits...

which brought it directly into line with Gaitskell's position.[20]

Sometime during August a possible list of ideal signatories was added to one of the copies being posted between Oxford and London. It read: Francis Place, William Lovett, Robert Owen, G.J. Holyoake, William Cooper, Henry George, William Morris, Robert Blatchford and Sidney Webb. On Crosland's copy the name Eduard Bernstein was added.

Crosland played no part in the public launch of the CDS because the organisers were intent that the public face of the campaign would be as grass-roots' as possible. He attended the planning meetings, recommended people as prospective Parliamentary candidates and helped in drafting circulars but his main contribution to the running of the campaign was in suggesting and contributing to the CDS newsletter *Campaign* and as a platform speaker.

CAMPAIGN

Keeping CDS supporters in touch and trying to match CND organisationally were aspects of CDS activity that could be described as 'practical politics". The other side to the conflict with the left and indeed the conflict with the Conservatives was winning the ideological argument. The main weapons the CDS employed to get its ideology across were *Campaign* and the contributions supporters made to the revisionist journal *Socialist Commentary*. The idea of a newsletter emerged from the early planning discussions. Tony Crosland, Philip Williams and Bill Rodgers worked out the details in November and December 1960.

> As Tony will have told you, we want to produce the first issue of 'Campaign' – which is what the newsletter is to be called – on or about 1st January. It will deal mainly with defence and the constitutional question... It is easier at the moment to visualise what it may look like than to describe it. There is general agreement that there should be as many short pieces as possible, including quotations from friends and enemies. The one point in principle raised was whether we should limit ourselves to replying to the left or whether we should try to be anti-Tory at the same time. This was resolved by agreeing that our anti-Toryism should be implicit

but that it should be reinforced by, for example, quotations from the speeches of the people we were running for the NEC.[21]

Campaign was run and written by Crosland and a committee whose membership included the other MPs Tom Bradley, Patrick Gordon Walker and Roy Jenkins. Non-MPs who did much of the writing included Tony King, Philip Williams, Michael Shanks, David Marquand, Bernard Donoughue and Anthony Dumont. The objective of *Campaign* was limited. It was not designed to take on *Tribune,* which as a long-established Labour weekly had a wide circulation, and it was beyond the resources of the CDS to produce anything as ambitious. It was designed to be the internal newsletter of the CDS and as such it provided a great deal of useful information and analysis. Crosland wrote some of the articles, organised others and contributed ideas and themes. He also spoke on CDS platforms, putting the leadership case for multilateralism and he was always a hit.

CDS tried to match CND and the left with its meetings and organised a series of special multilateralist events for the under-25s. The first of these took place in April 1962. The two-day school was directed by Dick Taverne with Brian Walden, Tyrell Burgess and Alan Day as speakers. This was followed up in January 1963 by a one-day school boldly entitled 'Creating the New Society", addressed by Tom Bradley on 'The Role of Trade Unions' and Tony Crosland on his follow up to *The Future of Socialism, The Conservative Enemy.* This school was directed by Brian Walden and attended by 73 young Labour supporters. Tony Crosland was a considerable success, with many people assuring Rodgers that they would attend again if they could be sure that Crosland was to speak.[22] A young Oliver Walston, then one of the leading members of CDS at Cambridge University, reviewed the school in a letter to Rodgers: 'Bradley was good but pedestrian in the morning. Crosland was provocative, rude, arrogant, brilliant, witty and outspoken.'[23]

At the outset of the Campaign, Crosland had assured Walden that money would not be a problem and he was as good as his word. He approached Jack Diamond, who had helped him with his research into the cooperative movement, for funds in August 1960 and Diamond was happy to oblige, becoming the crucial figure in financing the activity of CDS.[24]

The involvement with CDS came at a time in Crosland's life when a number of personal and political factors combined. Divorced from his first wife and not yet settled with Susan, he occupied a lieutenant's position in the party, while being the dominant intellectual personality of the revisionist wing. Earlier, Gaitskell had not been sufficiently threatened to merit a grass-roots' organisation dedicated to his protection, later the revisionists lost the leadership and the urge to organise at grass-roots' level. Crosland was then a contingent factionalist and his involvement did not alter his personal style nor influence his convictions on policy. He worked with small groups, he was a committee attender and drafter but he did not use CDS as a way of cultivating a faction of his own, people followed, as John Vaizey put it, because of his brain. When the ideas were not enough they stopped following. As Dick Taverne remembered, 'Tony Crosland was the great inspiration before I got into Parliament and the great disappointment afterwards'.[25] Looking closely at what he did with CDS, it is clear that in those activities that involved ideas and communicating those ideas he was central, but in the forging of an organisation and group identity, he was separate, part aloof and part resistant to surrendering himself to the collective experience. The clearest examples of his holding back were over Europe and the leadership election after Gaitskell's death.

On Europe, some of the CDS organisers, who had not been particularly pro-Community at the outset, went with the will of the majority of the group. Bill Rodgers, for example, went from lukewarmness towards the EEC to passionate advocacy, not only because of the merit of the case but because of a feeling of loyalty to the group and the policy which most of its members favoured. In this, they were being consistent. They had insisted at the outset that the CDS would not simply be Gaitskell's private army and the only time this insistence was tested, Rodgers was determined to uphold it. Crosland was happy to follow his leader on Europe, though he was not as set against the European Community at the outset as he was to be later. Over the leadership election, things were a little different. Here loyalty to the group went against the personal and political instincts of many and the Callaghan candidature, though hardly the gross disloyalty it was alleged to be by the Brownites, was, nevertheless, the undoing of the coherence of the Gaitskellites. With the leader dead, factions within the faction opened. Crosland was utterly dismissive of the need to support Brown simply because he was Gaitskell's old deputy. Some of the younger Gaitskellites shared his misgivings, but it was Rodgers who again served as the anchor for the 'true course". Crosland dismissed the case for Brown as nonsense, and in doing so, he cut many of the ties that bound the Gaitskellites to him, political cuts which were to deepen as the European issue came to define the self-perception of many social democrats.

CONCLUSION

It is not difficult to find personal parallels between New Labour ministers and the varying species of Old Labour that once roamed the political world. The current Deputy Prime Minister, John Prescott, is reminiscent of a sober George Brown – the political bruiser with roots in the movement–but he also has a strong streak of Barbara Castle's empire-building instincts. The current Chancellor of the Exchequer has something of the Stafford Cripps in him, being not so much at the treasury as becoming The Treasury, but there is also a hint of Denis Healey in his attitude that if he weren't there the whole edifice would collapse. Perhaps Robin Cook is the Roy Jenkins of his generation, always at slightly the wrong department to make a proper grab for the leadership. Tony Blair is not actually so difficult to place: the brilliance of Wilson circa 1963–4, is slowly evolving into the zeal of Gaitskell with a good dose of Nye Bevan's love of applause. But where, in all this, is the Tony Crosland? Where, in other words, does New Labour keep its brains?

Before the election, the answer might have been Frank Field, but he cares more about ideas than about the party. For Crosland there was no point in having one without the other; his relationship with the Labour Party, particularly his role in organising, reveals the ambiguity of his, and his generation of Labour revisionist intellectuals', position. Crosland as apparatchik, and the unlikely nature of that image, is one of the reasons we did not see New Labour a generation ago. The organising stopped dead for a decade after Hugh Gaitskell's death and by the time it started again the left had taken over the constituencies. In between, Crosland and other old revisionists redefined themselves as Ministers while Labour branches were overtaken by new generations of activists. The result – schism and the dominance of the party by the left – was an extended period in the wilderness. The emergence from that wilderness has seen, to a remarkable extent, a unity of intellectualism and activism, the apparatus once used for entryism is now used for modernisation and though a new centralism is creeping in, a democratised Labour Party is set to be more revisionist than the arch revisionist would ever have thought possible. That it did not come about much earlier is due to many wide-ranging reasons rooted in the political history of the last two decades, but might not part of the answer lie in the nature of Crosland as activist and the decision made to close down the CDS in 1964? My point is simple. CDS closed down after the 1964 election and the social democrats closed down their lobbying operation for a decade. The only front on which they fought was Europe and the cross-party nature of those struggles made them anathema to many Labour Party activists. In turn the left expended huge amounts of political energy organising campaigns on issues like unilateral nuclear disarmament that proved electoral liabilities. New Labour, at its best, combines the electorally astute intellectualism of the Gaitskellites, Jenkinsites – and, indeed, Croslandites – with the campaigning zeal and energy of the Bevanites and Bennites. Many of those now in the forefront of the party cut their teeth fighting each other in the years of confrontation. They now work in harmony, all having accepted the need for ideology to be subordinate to electoral strategy. Quite what Tony Crosland would have made of this unity of purpose and organisation is difficult to say, but he might have asked: what kind of society is being created?

Notes

1. Brivati(1996), chapters 15 and 16.
2. Summerskill and Brivati (1993), p.30.
3. *New Left Review*, 1(1) (1960), p.18.
4. CDS Papers: Untitled File, Walden to Pickstock (18 May 1960).
5. Pearce,(1991),p 2.
6. CDS Papers: Untitled File, Walden to Pickstock (18 May 1960) p. 1.
7. CDS Papers: Rodgers' CDS History File, p. 4.

8. CDS Papers: Rodgers' CDS History File p. 13.
9. CDS Papers: Rodgers' CDS History File, p. 8.
10. CDS Paper: Rodgers' CDS History File, p. 6.
11. 'The Campaign for Democratic Socialism, Witness Seminar,' *Contemporary Record* (Autumn 1993).
12. CDS Papers: Untitled File, Walden to Pickstock (18 May 1960).
13. CDS Papers: Untitled File, Williams to Crosland, undated.
14. CDS Papers: Manifesto Texts File: First Draft.
15. CDS Papers: Origins and Manifesto Text Files.
16. CDS Papers: Signatories File, Fourth Draft by Frank Pickstock after further discussion.
17. CDS Papers: Signatories File, 7th draft discussed at London meeting (29 July 1960).
18. CDS Papers: Signatories File, Fifth Draft, Crosland's in response to Fourth Draft by Pickstock.
19. CDS Papers: Origins File, Minute of meeting (25 September 1960).
20. CDS Papers: Manifesto File *A Manifesto Addressed to the Labour Movement*, paragraph 11.
21. CDS Papers: Editorial Committee, Rodgers to Williams (25 November 1960).
22. CDS Papers: Under-25s Conference January 1963, Rodgers to Crosland (7 January 1963).
23. CDS Papers: Under-25s General Correspondence, Walston to Rodgers (7 January 1963).
24. For full details see Brian Brivati (1996), pp. 384–5 and CDS Papers: Origins File, Minute of meeting (28 August 1960), Point 7, Officers and Finance.
25. 'The Campaign for Democratic Socialism, Witness Seminar', *Contemporary Record*, 7(2) (Autumn 1993), p 371.

References

Brian Brivati (1992) 'Tony Crosland and Campaign for Democratic Socialism, 1960–64', unpublished PhD, University of London.
Brian Brivati (1996) *Hugh Gaitskill* (Richard Cohen Books).
Robert Pearce (ed.) (1991) *Patrick Gordon Walker Political Diaries 1932–1971* (Historians' Press).
Michael Summerskill and Brian Brivati (1993) *The Group, 1954–1960: The Time of Hope* (Michael Summerskill, 1993).

11 Anthony Crosland as a Political Economist*
David Reisman

Returning to Trinity in the year of Attlee's new dawn, converting from Classics to PPE at the age of 27, the ex-paratrooper on his way to a First made a careful study of Marshall's *Principles*, Pigou's *Economics of Welfare* and Keynes' *General Theory* under the guidance of the pragmatic Robert Hall, whose *Economic System in a Socialist State* had in 1937 looked with Hayek to market pricing for accurate calculation even as it had looked with Jay, Dalton and Macmillan's *Middle Way* to the purposive nationalisation of the commanding heights. Crosland in 1947 replaced his tutor (invited to succeed James Meade as Economic Advisor to the Government) as Lecturer in Economics at Trinity. His principal scholarly contributions – 'The Movement of Labour in 1948' 'and (1949) Prices and Costs in Nationalised Undertakings' (1950) – demonstrate the lack of interest of a morally-minded socialist who had joined Labour at the age of 16 in the use of mathematics, diagrams and abstractions that do so little for the cause of equality and welfare. Later articles in *Encounter*, *Socialist Commentary* and *Tribune*, together with the polemical *Britain's Economic Problem* in 1953, show him more comfortable with economics when freed from the disciplinary detachment of arid formalism.

In 1950 the House took over from the College and the short five years in academic economics came for ever to an end. Crosland told his selection meeting in South Gloucestershire what his Oxford colleagues must long have suspected, that he saw economics as

---
* Written for this volume.

indispensable but boring, as 'a dreary & dismal subject...but one that grows more vital & important every day' (c.1949). By 'The Transition to Socialism' in the *New Fabian Essays* of 1952 – he returned to the managerial revolution and the new-style capitalism without capitalists in 'The Private and Public Corporation in Great Britain', published in E.S. Mason's *The Corporation in Modern Society* in 1959 – he had become a theorist of organisational behaviour whose interest in textbook economics was minimal. In 1956 there was *The Future of Socialism*. A revision of the basis–superstructure nexus to separate out social distance and social policy from the classical Marxism of capital and labour, it is remarkable for its singular indifference to the technicalities and potentialities that Crosland had addressed while an economics don. Gain-seeking enterprise managed by a dentist-like State was demonstrably capable of delivering the goods: 'The contemporary mixed economy is characterised by high levels both of employment and productivity and by a reasonable degree of stability' (1956, p.69). The economy had matured and the society had not. What the imbalance meant for the cause of reform was to Crosland clear enough: 'The long-run problems of concern to Socialists are no longer mainly economic ... It is sociologists that the party needs.' (1955a, p.6).

Crosland after Oxford was a practical politician who emphasised the instrumental value of sociological investigation. Yet he was also a trained economist, schooled in the economic exploitation of mid-Victorian capitalism and a witness at first hand to the chronic market failure of the 1930s. In directing attention to sociology, Crosland the politician was not saying (with Galbraith) that acquisition and materialism were no longer serious subjects for inquiry, only that absolute poverty and relative deprivation had become the new priorities for the social interventionist anxious to do good.

Crosland after Oxford was a politician with an interest in sociology. Yet he was also a trained economist, exposed as a voracious reader to the sociological economics of Bernstein and Schumpeter and as a socially-committed undergraduate to the debate about market versus State that had been a core issue for pre-mathematical economists like Malthus and Mill. Systemic holists like Smith and Marx had resisted an excessive division of scholarly labour in favour of the multidisciplinary synthesis that Crosland found so revealing in wide-ranging works like Lewis' *Theory of Economic Growth*: 'It needed a book like this to make one realise just how circumscribed a subject economics had become. This was certainly not always so; all the great economists, from Adam Smith to Marx, automatically took the whole of the social sciences as their province' (1955b, p.10). Crosland by the 1950s had become a part of that heterodoxy. Attracted by social vision and repelled by blinkered formalism, he had opted for political economy because technical economics did not shed sufficient light.

The systemic holists had situated the economy in its broader context. They had not denied its importance – or under-rated its dynamic. *The Wealth of Nations*, *Capital*, *Evolutionary Socialism*, *Capitalism, Socialism and Democracy* all have this in common, that they postulate a close causal link between economic evolution and the institutional development which follows in its wake. *The Future of Socialism* is a horse from the same venerable stable. Crosland was not an economic determinist who believed that socialism would inevitably be the by-product of growth. What he was instead was a democrat and a realist, aware that growth could foster the complacent conservatism of 'you've never had it so good' but that without growth there would be insufficient support for public expenditure paid for through taxation: 'Rapid growth is an essential condition of any significant re-allocation of resources' (1971, p.75). Growth generates the resources even if it does not predestine them. In his emphasis upon growth as in his expectation of interdependence, Crosland in his political economy was clearly the heir to the systemic holists who by the time of *The Future of Socialism* were more and more being read exclusively as the history of economic thought. Hardly any economics undergraduates doing degrees in the country of Crosland's birth now see the need to open the great books of Smith and Marx, of Schumpeter – and of Crosland himself. One consequence is that the political economy tradition, synthetic and evolutionary, must be regarded as a window on the world in real danger of being closed.

Crosland said that 'the rate at which we increase public spending must be related to our overall rate of economic growth' (1976, p.14). Crosland said 'must' and he meant 'must'. His political economy must stand or fall on the extent to which his recommendations, accelerating the rise in *per capita* living standards, may be expected to produce a surplus for redistribution without pain.

Thus the taxes that can be levied are clearly constrained by the need to expand. Crosland was writing at the time of the 83% (and, with the 15% surcharge on the 'unearned' elements of interest and dividends, the 98%) highest marginal rates of personal income-tax that many left-wingers still welcomed as a mode of levelling through chopping down. A strong advocate of the infrastructure of opportunity, a philosophical moderate persuaded that the improvement in education, healthcare, housing and income maintenance would not be possible without the *sine qua non* of enterprise and assiduity, Crosland warned the confiscators that their socialism of levelling down was a threat to the more constructive socialism of positive-sum empowerment that sustained growth would be in a position to facilitate. Emphasising incentives, he said that a reduction rather than an increase would in truth be the socialist way where lower tax-rates were needed for 'individual effort and enterprise' (1956, p.246) and an increase would mean that 'equality begins to react really seriously on the supply of ability' (1956, p.145). His endorsement of net differentials 'wider than most socialists would consider "just" (1956, p.226) would be an admission that the principle is equity but the meta-principle affluence were it not for the fact that economic growth, 'a definite socialist objective' (1956, p.223) in its own right, is also a 'precondition of a decent social sector' (1962, p.24) that a distortion of the market-determined pay structure would make it more difficult to put in place. Should pay based on power and seniority predominate over pay set flexibly by shortage and productivity, should higher taxes cause households to supply more labour and not to demand more leisure, should the social sector favour the haves (on the model of university education) and not the have-nots (on the model of income support), the consistent Croslandite would, of course, have carefully to re-think the proposition that direct taxation must be limited in the interests of equality and welfare made acceptable through maximal growth.

In the case of corporation tax, Crosland sought to promote economic growth not through containment but through re-direction. Absolutely clear about the profit motive – 'the rationale of business activity in any society, whether capitalist or socialist, which is growing and dynamic' (1956, p.16) – he believed nonetheless that a two-tier tax was needed to encourage the profit-seekers to curb dividend payments and to re-invest in plant. His proposal shows a lack of faith in the market for capital which is at variance with his more usual defence of economic efficiency as the product of economic self-interest. Nor is it certain that his interventionism will engineer its desired outcome. Ploughing back can retard growth where it retains in low-return giants (taken without demonstration by Crosland, like Galbraith, as the powerhouse of development and change) the venture capital needed by risk-taking new entrants in sunrise sectors. There is also a certain inequity in granting a tax exemption to the re-investment of the large when no equivalent subsidy is promised for the new investment of the unincorporated. If fiscal welfare is indeed required for capital accumulation, it would make more sense for the concessions to be offered directly to savers (the TESSAs and PEPs of Mrs Thatcher's capitalism) and not to some or all of the businesses in which the households invest. If fiscal welfare is not in the event required to stimulate the needed flows of savings and investment, it would make even more sense for the State to specialise in socialism while leaving capital accumulation to private prudence.

Crosland made growth his explicit maximand in respect of income and of corporation tax. The relationship between growth and tax is less clear in the case of his proposals for the treatment of wealth. Capital gains tax damps down destabilising speculation and accelerating turn-around – but it also interferes with rational arbitrage and the market equilibration of asset values. An annual wealth tax creams off a proportion of accounts and shares that had found a productive outlet – and it skews surviving holdings towards non-mercantile stocks such as paintings which are not made subject to tax. Estate duties nationalise a part of savings at death (a partial disincentive to abstain from consumption while alive) – and the Death Duty Commissioners are instructed to invest with a view to social as well as rate-of-return considerations (a possible cause of resource transfer from go-ahead employment creators to declining areas and loss-making enterprises). In relation to economic growth and to economic growth alone, the possibility must be acknowledged that such taxes will combat the perceived evil of unequal outcomes at the price of the economic resources that are needed to equalise opportunities at the start of the race.

Crosland did not see the levelling of assets as a major source of public finance. The annual wealth tax was desirable 'on strictly social or redistributive grounds' (1962, p.23) and not because of its potential as an earner of revenue. The capital gains tax was attractive not because of the funds it would raise but because of the tall trees it would prune back towards the median: 'The yield would probably never be enormous, but the case for it, on grounds of both equity between individuals and equality between classes, is overwhelming' (1956, p.243). Crosland, at the time when Denis Healey was promising taxes designed 'to make the rich howl in agony', expressed his support for a greater burden on the prosperous as a means of building a consensus around Labour's new social compact:

> This will not release huge sums of money to help the poor; the spending of the rich in total is not high enough for that. But without such a redistribution we shall not command the moral authority to carry through our social programme. (1974b)

Crosland is not saying that the pruning back is predictably a cause of faster growth or that the sums released are the indispensable transfers that make possible the equalisation of life-chances. What he is saying is that pruning back is a focus for legitimacy and a catalyst for 'moral authority'. It is not clear what 'moral authority' can possibly be derived from the symbolic bullying of an envied minority. Crosland's more usual insistence upon positive-sum expansion is, all things considered, a much healthier – and more important – element in his political economy of the middle ground.

Crosland's political economy must stand or fall on the extent to which his recommendations may be expected to contribute to rapid growth. The previous section considered taxes and tax rates. The present section turns to education and training.

Well-resourced schools rescue potential meritocrats from wasteful under-performance and diffuse the lower-level skills that will be required by the beta-material. The abolition of the 11+ reduces the chance that late developers will fall through the net because of a once-for-all sift that is biased and unreliable. The comprehensive institution promotes uninhibited mixing that exposes future bosses to the values and feelings of the future rank-and-file. The binary system improves access to vocational qualifications by means of day-release and evening education in a local polytechnic. In ways such as these, it is clear, Crosland intended that educational policy should be economic policy as well. Social equality can evidently be good business, socialism the complement to capitalism, in a society that invites its State to train.

Crosland did not consider the possibility that the cost could be shared, either with businesses (via a skills levy or a statutory training commitment) or with households (via loans rather than grants or a graduate tax on a blatantly regressive subsidy). Where the cost can be so shifted, of course, the State would not be in the ambiguous position of inflating the returns for multinationals and young stockbrokers by means of a resource injection that would have produced more equity and more growth alike if it had not so much replaced the spending of private-sector gain-seekers as augmented the spending of the absolutely deprived. Le Grand and others show that the middle classes absorb a disproportionate share of public services like education and health. Goldthorpe and others show that public services since 1945 have done little to alter the traditional relationships between origins and destinations. Evidence like this suggests that the alpha-material was being paid a high-return subsidy, that the beta-material was under-consuming the push that it needed for upward mobility. Crosland in pursuit of classlessness and of dynamism alike would therefore have done well to have developed further his interest in discriminatory targeting along the lines of Plowden's Educational Priority Areas in preference to an across-the-board universalism made legitimate by the diagnosis that 'the division in Britain is due mainly to our educational system' (1962, p.210n.) that with hindsight appears too simple, too comfortable, too optimistic.

Crosland, a lapsed lecturer in market economics, expressed the view that individual choice in the sense of Mill was to be ranked above communal banding in the sense of Durkheim:

> the values of solidarity, community, and even traditional neighbourliness may well threaten the opposite (and equally 'socialist'!) values of freedom, autonomy and critical revolt ... I personally hold the latter values higher. (1962, p.210)

Thus it was that Crosland, hostile as he was to the head start on sale to the affluent through the public schools, could not in the end bring himself to press for their nationalisation: 'A democracy cannot forbid people to found schools and charge for going to them' (cited in S. Crosland, 1982, p.149). The clients of the State sector who might not have wanted compulsory integration in the comprehensive schools (or who might have feared a fall in educational standards such as would *de facto* make comprehensive-leavers less attractive to economic employers) were not to be offered an equivalent measure of tolerant self-determination: 'If it's the last thing I do, I'm going to destroy every fucking grammar school in England' (cited in S. Crosland, 1982, p.148). The rule was evidently to be Keynes-like wise leadership in the political exchange nexus, Friedman-like mix and match in the paying, shopping sector. It would have been more equitable to have allowed parents in both sectors (perhaps making use of league tables, conspicuous differentiation, means-tested education vouchers) to enjoy the same 'freedom, autonomy and critical revolt' that the customers of the public schools already enjoy in respect of educational services. The implications for economic dynamism could be at least as significant for Crosland's political economy as would be the universalisation of consumer sovereignty. Parents, directly involved in selection and keen to see their children succeed, could actually make education an even more effective contributor to the process of economic growth.

Culture as well as skill can have an impact on productivity. Crosland said little about the hidden curriculum which, through the inculcation of assiduity, independence, punctuality, accuracy, deferred gratification, competition and cooperation, is so important an output of the child socialisation industry. He could arguably have taken a stronger stand against permissive and undisciplined attitudes which impose burdens on others, against the decay in the work ethic which he was too much a graduate of the Plymouth Brethren ever fully to comprehend. Even so, Crosland was undeniably an economist who had a social psychologist's appreciation of cultural values. Nowhere is this more apparent than in the many passages where Crosland shows himself so critical of the 'smug, lethargic conservatism' (1960, p.223) that, freezing out novelty, was holding Britain back.

Of course there is a youthful openness to discovery in Crosland's attraction to American hot jazz in preference to the stuffiness of a rigid and stratified status quo that had never had it so dull. Yet there is economic growth as well as temperamental restlessness in

Crosland's defence of vibrant alertness against the wet blanket of comparative statics. The unions were in a rut of confrontation and demarcation. The manufacturers were too complacent, too afraid of innovation. The nation as a whole was thinking equilibrium because it lacked the imagination to be thinking change. Crosland contended that people in Britain needed to dynamise their culture if they were indeed to speed up their growth.

Attitudes had to be liberalised; and a capitalist market, 'as competitive as possible' (c.1950), was a more powerful agency even than American television or politicians' exhortations. The abolition of resale price maintenance would expose shopkeepers to the cold shower of rivalry. Restrictive practices legislation would force oligopolists to defend their mergers and cartels with arguments more other-regarding than the producers' wish for a quiet life. Membership in EFTA (and, with less enthusiasm, the EEC) would substitute for cosy accommodation the challenge of 'keen competition from imports' (1969, p.238). De-regulation of opening-times and of theatrical proprieties would release the kaleidoscope of adaptations that was being immobilised by convention. Union reform was not an option (practical politics evidently ruled out the strike ballots and cooling-off periods of a later cohort of pro-marketeers); and Crosland's espousal of new restrictions to replace the old – 'God alone cannot create an Alkali Inspectorate or stop the barbaric depredations of profit-hungry property firms' (1971, p.85) – suggests that it would be premature for the conservative enemy to concede defeat. Still, however, it is clear that Crosland wanted attitudinal capital to embrace permanent revolution and that he looked to the competitive market to produce Marx-like the ethos that would produce Smith-like the growth.

Observers who associate socialism more with fellowship than with entrepreneurship will welcome the resources for welfare but will question the self-seeking individualism upon which free enterprise relies. Certainly the values and aspirations are closer to those of currency speculators and estate agents than they are to the teachers and social workers whose motivation has traditionally exemplified the socialist standard of community service. Crosland was not unaware that he was appealing to non-socialist vices in order to finance the public good. One way in which he sought to reconcile the (debased) deontology with the (beneficent) consequentialism was to invoke the economies of size which were putting paid meritocrats in charge of private-sector businesses. Thus the organisational revolution had resulted in a cult of group activity, an ideology of collective responsibility, which was a world away from the selfish acquisitiveness of the classical owner-accumulator: 'Decision-making is more and more passing from the individual to the team' (1956, p.19). The management-run giant, again, had become increasingly prepared to settle for the live-and-let-live of historic share and fixprice accommodation in preference to the cut-throat ruthlessness from which only the passive shareholders could hope to derive any benefit: 'Most people would agree that Britain to-day is a markedly less competitive society than it was a century ago' (1956, p.69). Control by salaried bureaucrats, oligopoly as mutual aid – the implication for the economy is a fair profit well below the attainable profit, a price charged 'well below the market or profit-maximising price' (1956, p.17). Thus does capitalism become more socialist even as socialism acknowledges capitalism to be the agency that pays for the interventionism.

Crosland was aware that profit-seeking ranked above social duty is the most usual interpretation of capitalism's productive performance, of the market's efficient flexibility. He must also have appreciated that a self-denying price set below the market-clearing price can be a cause of under-production on the side of supply, frustration and queueing on the side of demand. It is not ideal in the circumstances that Crosland took the new-style sleepiness to mean that capitalism was 'becoming humanised' (1956, p.18) when the truth is that it was simply becoming conservative. In opting for a mixed ethos of market fellowship in tandem with market entrepreneurship, Crosland was clearly trying both to have his socialist cake and to eat his capitalist growth. Half a tiger is not, however, much of a tiger at all. It would arguably have been better for Crosland to have encouraged the gain-seekers to go all out for return in order in that way to maximise the fiscal increment that could be collected by the State.

The bias was in favour of the market. The exceptions confirm that social democracy is the language of pragmatism. Crosland believed that free enterprise was the most dependable source of growth. He also saw a role for nationalisation and regulation where the facts suggested that the State would be the more economical agency.

Thus, in respect of nationalisation, Crosland recommended an open mind:

> I have long believed that no generalisation was possible about the relative efficiency of publicly-owned and privately-owned industry. Each case has to be considered pragmatically on its merits.
> (1974c, p.v)

The advocates of Clause Four had defended State ownership with a range of arguments which Crosland dismissed as irrelevant – the end to labour's exploitation (yet workers are protected by their unions and profits are indispensable for reinvestment); the redistribution of the national income (yet welfare and taxes are more finely-tuned to need, while the British government is the largest single employer of low-waged labour); the promotion of a cooperative atmosphere in industry (yet miners and railwaymen still go on strike and pollution control is blocked by manual grades afraid of the threat to jobs). Least of all was Crosland convinced (he pointed frequently to the poor performance of the Soviet-type economies) that an expanded State position in the basic means of production would be likely to improve productivity or to raise the rate of growth: 'The efficiency criterion ... does not point clearly to further large-scale nationalisation.' (1959, p.274). The advocates of Clause Four were far too confident that theirs was a universal panacea. Recommending an open mind, Crosland concluded that nationalisation was in truth no more than one microeconomic option among many.

The great wave of nationalisations had probably come to an end. Even so, Crosland believed, the transfer of title that had already occurred had unquestionably delivered an economic payoff. Coordinated direction had reduced wasteful duplication in the case of coal. Pump-priming investment had made possible economies of scale in the case of steel. Telecommunications and other utilities had been prevented from abusing their natural monopoly. State-owned Renault and Volkswagen had upgraded the performance of the laggard private sector 'by the force of example and competition' (1961b, p.42). In the future the government should not hesitate to nationalise selectively, picking winners, buying up inefficient firms, putting losers back on their feet. It should also explore the nationalisation of development land (the demand-determined rise in value serving as a beacon to destabilising speculation) and of the unfurnished rental sector (the private landlord in the era of rent control having demonstrably failed to satisfy the consumers' requirements). In ways such as these, Crosland argued, the State should continue to employ the purchase of title as a policy instrument sensitively directed towards a perceived market failure. Overall, however, Crosland was persuaded that the great wave of across-the-board nationalisations had probably come to an end.

The most urgent justification for State ownership was economic performance. Crosland's case for nationalisation was evidently derived from his commitment to economic growth and with it to economic efficiency. Ideally, therefore, he should have balanced his socialisation with a promise of re-privatisation should commercial capitalism re-emerge as the better buy. Thus the new technology in telecommunications would have to be seen as re-introducing active competition into an industry that had evolved beyond its single-firm status; while bureaucratic inertia ossified into indifference to the consumer's convenience would have to be taken as a reminder that shareholders' watchfulness and the threat of bankruptcy can be a more effective source of accountability even than the Standing Committee. Crosland was always quick to emphasise that the nationalised industries should adopt a productive and not a redistributive maximand. He defended the arms'-length autonomy of management in the State sector; proposed that new investment should normally be paid for out of internally-generated revenues; championed the supply-and-demand price over the non-market-clearing price. The nationalised industries, Crosland maintained, had to be regarded as businesses and could never be mistaken for social services. That being the case, he should ideally have put forward a socialist's promise of re-privatisation where economic performance would improve as a result.

Publicly owned or privately owned, economic agencies irrespective of their sector remain subject to the authority of the law. Regulation in that way can be employed to impose the nation's priorities without any need for the transfer of title. A practising politician, a conviction pragmatist, a managerial theorist at ease with power divorced from capital, Crosland found the compromise of statute an attractive halfway house between market without mandate and command by plan.

Regulation in the sense of Crosland can in some cases be compared not to an investment good but to living off wealth. What the consumption strategy would mean is that the nation through its legislators would decide to spend some of its growth not on better schools and roads but on non-productive end-states that would improve the quality of life. The control of noise-pollution is a case in point where the gain in final satisfaction is only secured through a redirection of resources: 'We must accept higher prices if we compel manufacturers to design quieter engines' (c.1969–70). Crosland in office blocked plans for new London airports at Stansted and Maplin; and he was in favour of protecting historic buildings like Norman Shaw's Scotland Yard even though a modern tower-block would almost certainly have boosted the economic throughput of a centrally-situated plot. Crosland never under-estimated the attractions of town and country planning, of health and safety protection. What he did make clear, however, is that the bias is in favour of the market – and that a nation cannot spend on amenity without the cushion of growth.

Crosland in the circumstances devoted disproportionate attention to regulation that had the character not of final utility but of a productive input. One illustration would be his support for George Brown's National Plan of 1964: modelled on the French experience with indicative planning, it would coordinate business expectations and thereby make more effective the capitalist market sector. Another illustration would be his invocation to the Monopolies and Mergers Commission not to throw out with the combinations bent on dominance and manipulation those socially beneficial mergers which are essential for technological advance:

> In general, mergers are desirable if they lead to better management or genuine economies of scale without eliminating workable competition. In my view, more often than not, in Britain mergers will fulfil this condition. (1969, pp. 235–6)

It can even happen that the private sector lacks the imagination and the initiative to bring about the rationalisation that is required to cover the overheads of research and development. The nation as a whole would be the beneficiary of the invention and the innovation that the private capitalists are too timid to bring within the choice-set. That is why, should big business be too backward to become big enough, the State must itself take the lead in marrying up the capitals. Crosland praised the pro-active Industrial Reorganisation Corporation for doing just that, for 'doing an excellent job in restructuring many sectors of British industry' (1969, p. 236).

Sometimes the merger should be initiated. Sometimes it should be allowed. Sometimes it should be prevented. Always, however, it should be scrutinised with a view to economic performance:

> I see no inconsistency in showing concern about the possible detriment to the public interest of monopoly power, while at the same time working actively for stronger industrial units, because they are both means to the common end of industrial efficiency.
> (1968, col.454)

Ranking eclecticism above rules and outcomes above processes, Crosland in that way was relegating rigid dogmas to the status of the conservative enemy. Efficiency leading to expansion was to be the guiding light in the formulation of microeconomic policy. A growth-funded socialism would be putting at risk the prospects for council housing and respectable pensions where it, becoming too imaginative, relied too heavily upon any other.

Nationalisation and regulation can contribute to economic growth. So can the management of total demand. Macroeconomic policy to social democrats who had lived through the inter-war years, the marches from Jarrow, the promise of the dictatorships, symbolised the ultimate victory of the Keynesian commitment to full employment over the Marxian prediction of stagnation, destitution and crisis. Full employment (politically a vote-winner and ethically the precondition for industrious self-reliance) ensured that productive potential did not disappear into involuntary idleness. Discretionary tinkering set wise technocrats free from the market automaticity that had produced the 1930s. Both the capacity operation and the leaderly pragmatism appealed strongly to Anthony Crosland, convinced as he was that counter-cyclical intervention could and should be trusted to protect the macro-economy from the nightmare scenario of unemployment benefits drawn where value-added ought to have been supplied.

The spectre being the demand shortfall, the postwar Keynesians had a bias in favour of public expenditure which added a macroeconomic endorsement to the reformers' call for State services to correct a microeconomic failing. Crosland was the heir to both strands of the defence. As a socialist he supported 'a relative transfer of resources from private consumption to public expenditure' within the context of a growing pool (which would reduce or eliminate the consumers' sense of loss) because he was of the opinion that welfare would alleviate distress and infrastructure facilitate expansion: 'Equality and higher public expenditure are what divide us from the Tories' (1974a, pp. 26,8).

As a Keynesian he believed that public investments and public transfers – pyramid-building on Salisbury Plain as much as the construction of new comprehensives in the deprived inner-city – were needed to countervail the ever-present tendency towards underconsumption which as late as the Macmillan boom was still seen by many as capable of restoring the involuntary unemployment that had been a constant element throughout Crosland's formative years. Keynes in any case had legitimated the budget deficit. Few gifts can be more valuable to the high-spending interventionist, to the advocate of public sector leverage, than the authorisation to separate the pleasure of current benefit from the pain of future payment.

Crosland as a *political* economist cannot have been entirely oblivious to the temptations faced by a voter-pleasing government in consequence of the licence to fund spending out of bond-issue and not out of tax. Himself a creature of election and re-election, he must have been aware of the scope for opportunistic Machiavellianism such as is imputed by public-choice thinkers like Downs and Buchanan to popularity-maximising democrats who know that the generations burdened with the service and the repayment will not see through the illusion (or even mature into a vote) until a new set of political leaders has inherited the poisoned chalice. Crosland as a political *economist* cannot have been entirely unaware of the possibility that the national debt would crowd out private sector investment projects; that the competition for limited savings would force up the interest rate; that debt-related costs would represent an ever-increasing share of the higher public spending that the social democrats so much wanted to bring about. A politician and an economist both, Crosland must have known about the temptations even as he could anticipate the escalation. It is striking in the circumstances that he had so little to say about the worst-case threat which to some would suggest a mandatory balanced budget. The reason is probably of a moral nature. Crosland was a public-spirited Gaitskellite who had invested his self-image in *pro bono publico*. He found it difficult to imagine that his fellow Parliamentarians, justifiably known as *Honourable* Members, would knowingly do what was irresponsible or wrong. A later generation, more cynical about sleaze and less confident about economic management, will not necessarily share his Tawney-like conviction that good politicians will do good things and that an involved electorate will see through the false promises and the personal ambitions of bad ones.

The post-war Keynesians feared the shortfall in demand that would return the economy to recession. High spenders like Crosland were not prepared for the distortion of market signals and the arbitrary redistribution of incomes of an inflationary Britain in which full employment appeared to be incompatible with price stability. Always stronger on a rise in demand to expand real variables than he was on a cut in demand to contain nominal values, Crosland says little about the control of the money supply, let alone about deflationary tax increases, about an end to the public expenditure ratchet, about the textbook budget surplus once excess capacity has demonstrably been exhausted. His indifference to the suppression of demand-pull inflation, painful though such a commitment would be to a welfare Keynesian attracted by taxes on the rich that fall in part on savings and by equalising services that increase the pressure on supply, in effect puts full employment itself at risk from anticipated wage and price spiralling such as serves as a stimulus to prolonged and speculative search.

Crosland's favourable attitude to a national policy on prices and incomes reflects his resistance to the squeeze and slow growth implicit in the Phillips Curve trade-off, to the reactive suddenness of the stop-go macroeconomics that had made it so difficult for business to plan: 'You can't expect industry to grow rapidly if you thwack it on the head whenever it does so' (1961a, p.67). An incomes policy was an acknowledgement of the institutional and cost-push elements in the allocative mechanism. It reconciled economic objectives by containing prices without creating unemployment. It allowed socialists the scope to discriminate in favour of the less-advantaged within the constraint of the overall ceiling. It complemented well the Social Contract in which higher pensions would march alongside wage restraint, maternity leave collaborate actively with prices kept below the level that the traffic would bear. The Social Contract was an appeal to solidarity, mutual aid and the spirit of Dunkirk: 'The Social Contract asks all of us to recognise our dependence on each other' (1975). It was also a counsel of desperation. Incomes policy in the Crosland sense was voluntary, unsupported by demand restraint, isolated from the macroeconomics of the world beyond the Cliffs, a deliberate distortion of the market-clearing vectors. Incomes policy appealed to Crosland as an economist in politics. Whether it would have made as much sense to him as an economist at Oxford must remain a matter for debate.

Much would depend on its efficacy as the means to an end. The political economy of Anthony Crosland is the analysis of the managed market in pursuit of the maximum attainable rate of growth. Crosland's socialism is to be found in the proposals he makes for social services and social engineering. Economics to Crosland was not the core of the socialist alternative in the way that it had been in the historic utopias of State planning, worker ownership, industrial democracy, the negation of the negation of surplus value, the classless mode of production that transcended the profit motive. Rather, economics was the instrument that maximised the gains from capitalism's triumph in order to make possible the transition to reform.

References

Works by C.A.R. Crosland

(c.1949) Speech to the selection-meeting in South Gloucestershire, unpublished ms, n.d., probably 1949, in Crosland Papers, British Library of Political and Economic Science, Box 13(21)
(1949) 'The Movement of Labour in 1958', *Bulletin of the Oxford Institute of Statistics*, 15.
(c.1950) 'The Nature of Capitalist Crisis', unpublished paper, n.d., probably 1950, in Crosland Papers, Box 13(23).
(1950) 'Prices and Costs in Nationalised Undertaxings', *Oxford Economic Papers*, 13.
(1955a) 'A Time for Hard Thinking', *The Observer*, 9 October.
(1955b) 'Out of the Rut', review of W.A. Lewis, *The Theory of Economic Growth*, *The Observer*, 6 November.
(1956) *The Future of Socialism* (Jonathan Cape), reprinted as Vol.VII in D.A. Reisman, (ed.), *Theories of the Mixed Economy* (Pickering & Chatto, 1994). All page-references in this chapter refer to the abridged edition, published by Jonathan Cape in 1964.
(1959) 'The Private and Public Corporation in Great Britain', in E.S. Mason, (ed.), *The Corporation in Modern Society* (Harvard University Press).
(1960) 'Smashing Things', *The Spectator*, 204, 12 February.
(1961a) 'On Economic Growth', *Encounter*, 15, April.
(1961b) 'The Role of Public Ownership', *Encounter*, 16, reprinted in his *The Conservative Enemy*,(1962).
(1962) *The Conservative Enemy* (Jonathan Cape).
(1968) Speech in the House of Commons, 20 March, in Parliamentary Debates (Hansard) Vol.761.
(1969) 'Monopolies and Mergers', in his *Socialism Now*, (1974).
(c.1969–70) Speech at a Guildhall banquet, unpublished ms, n.d., probably 1969–70, in Crosland Papers, Box 13(20) Pt. ii.
(1971),'A Social-Democratic Britain', *Fabian Tract* 404, reprinted in his *Socialism Now*(1974).
(1974a) *Socialism Now* (ed.) by D. Leonard (Jonathan Cape).
(1974b) Speech in Grimsby, 7 October, unpublished ms, in Crosland Papers, Box 13(29).

(1974c) 'Socialism, Land and Equality', *Socialist Commentary*, March.

(1975) Speech to the North Lincolnshire Society of Quantity Surveyors, 21 February, unpublished ms, in Crosland Papers, Box 13(31).

(1976) 'Battle for the Public Purse', *The Guardian*, 24 March.

Other reference

Crosland, S. (1982) *Tony Crosland* (Jonathan Cape).

12 Equality of Access*
Peter Kellner

Does New Labour believe in equality? The question sounds simple, but in fact it is not, which is one of the main reasons why no clear, convincing answer has been given. For although 'equality' is one of the most emotive words in the lexicon of centre-left politics, it has no settled or agreed meaning.

Ever since the cry went up during the French revolution for 'liberté, egalité, fraternité', the drive for a more equal society has inspired generations of reformers. Wherever they looked, they saw grotesque inequality, oppression, discrimination and hardship. In such circumstances the task of defining equality seemed irrelevant, almost absurd – like defining a racehorse in an empty paddock. You did not need to be an expert to spot its absence. Equality, whatever its precise meaning, demanded greater justice and a fairer distribution of power, wealth and income. Was the long-term ambition equality of outcome or merely equality of opportunity? How were they to be measured? To what extent did equality possess a civic and social, as well as an economic, dimension? Such questions might be theoretically real, but they had little bearing on practical politics. To be sure, the different definitions of 'equality' implied different eventual goals, but they were all far away and, for the time being, in roughly the same direction. So the immediate policies required to travel towards them were much the same – a full adult franchise, redistribution through the tax system, universal public services, laws

---
* Written for this volume.

against gender and race discrimination, and so on.

Anthony Crosland recognised the problem in *The Future of Socialism;* and he was honest enough to admit ducking the solution. After attacking the level of economic and social inequality in Britain, he continued:

> How far towards equality do we wish to go? I do not regard this as either a sensible or a pertinent question, to which one could possibly give, or should attempt to give, a precise reply. We need, I believe, more equality than we have now... We can therefore describe the direction of advance, and even discern the immediate landscape ahead; but the ultimate objective lies wrapped in complete uncertainty. (Chapter 7, section VIII)

That definition-free approach to equality is no longer sufficient. Society has changed, the terms of political debate have changed, the intellectual argument has changed. The principles of civic equality have now been established, if not always observed. Labour has formally abandoned redistribution through the tax and benefits system as a means of redressing inequality. And growing doubts have been expressed about the theoretical virtues – let alone practical possibilities – of both equality of outcome and equality of opportunity. If 'equality' is to remain part of the centre-left's lexicon as anything more than a sentimental genuflection to the past, its definition must be brought up to date.

In some ways, the Left's problems with equality today resemble its problems with state ownership during the 1980s. The Left railed (rightly) against untrammelled free markets and retained a symbolic devotion to the dream of common ownership. As long as the dream persisted – and long after much of Labour's leadership perceived its irrelevance to the modern world – the Left had difficulty contemplating other visions. By persuading Labour to change

Clause Four of its constitution in 1996, Tony Blair removed a block to fresh thinking about the role of markets, regulation, investment and ownership. The Left needs to rethink its approach to equality in much the same way as it has needed to rethink its approach to the ownership of the means of production, distribution and exchange. In the 1980s, the poverty of the Left's thinking on economic organisation allowed the free market Right to capture an ideological initiative. In the 1990s, the Left's failure so far to produce a robust definition of equality risks ceding the debate to those who deny that inequality matters. The purpose of this chapter is to suggest that a new definition of equality is available that is both relevant and robust. I have called it 'equality of access'. I believe that it avoids the pitfalls of both equality of outcome and equality of opportunity. 'Equality of access' provides a worthy ambition for a modern, reforming government. Applied sensibly, it could bring coherence to a wide range of policies, and provide a yardstick by which to measure their impact.

* * *

'Equality of access' is underpinned by three principles:
(1) equality, in its different facets, applies to everyone at all times: to rich and poor, to men and women, to black and white, to those who pass exams and those who fail them;
(2) when the principle of equality is invoked, it should be for its own sake, not merely as a stepping stone to some wider social objective;
(3) equality is ultimately about humanity, not money. In practice money often matters hugely, for equality of access is denied in many important areas to people who have too little; however, money is a means to an end, not the end itself.

Equality of access casts its net far wider than equality of outcome and equality of opportunity. It is concerned not just with the skills and material means that contented citizens need, but with information, power, security, health and justice. It is about rights at work and the freedom to walk through streets without fear. 'Equality of access' proposes that a mature democracy should strive for a range of equal membership rights for all its citizens, involving parity of access to those things that, together, comprise a just and healthy society. Here is a provisional list:

Everyone should have equality of access to...

- the ballot box
- the information that enables people to hold to account those who wield power, public and private, in their lives
- competent, affordable representation when in discussion or dispute with those who wield power
- safe and peaceful neighbourhoods
- fair treatment by the police and courts
- reasonable, affordable housing
- healthy, affordable food
- prompt and appropriate medical treatment when needed
- (for children and young adults) education that will enable people to achieve their full potential as adults
- (for adults) the means to generate an income, without detriment to dignity or health, that is sufficient to sustain a reasonable livelihood.

That list doubtless contains defects and omissions. However, it seeks to set out a range of issues in which (in the view of this writer, at least) equality has an intrinsic virtue. The most obvious example is the ballot box: every elector should have one vote. Equality of the franchise is the essence of democracy. Even here, though, the emphasis is on access rather than outcome. An elector may choose to abstain. Elections are decided by those who vote, not by those who stay away. The key thing is that every elector should have equal *access* to the ballot box; which is why we allow postal or proxy votes to those who are unable to attend the polling station in person on election day.

That is a relatively simple, uncontroversial example of equality of access, one which is applied to a large extent (though not completely: witness the difficulties many homeless people face when they seek to join the electoral register.) Others are more complex. Equality of access to information does not just concern central government, but local government, the public services and private business. There is obviously room for debate about how much information should be made available and what can reasonably be kept confidential. It is also, equally obviously, the case that some people will end up better informed than others – those who are determined to find things out will know more than those who cannot be bothered. But as with the ballot box, the primary issue is equality of access. Advances in technology offer enormous scope to make far more information available to more people; but the principle of equality of access would by violated if there develops an 'information under-class' of people whose circumstances deprive them of the chance to use this technology.

Or consider access to the means to generate an income. This covers both those who can work and those who cannot. Equality of access is designed to impose a duty, as well as convey a right, to people who have the capacity to earn an income. If able-bodied people turn down reasonable opportunities to work for reasonable pay, there is no reason why the rest of the community should pay for welfare benefits to save them from the consequences of their action. However, the community does have the responsibility to ensure that the means to earn a living are available and that employees are properly treated at work. Likewise with pensions. The community – in practice, the state – has a duty to design arrangements that ensure dignity and decent living standards in old age. These arrangements might involve a generous state pension, means-tested supplements, private pensions plans, or a combination of all three. Equality of access allows for responsibility to be shared. What matters is that access is universal, even if different people use different forms of access to secure a comfortable retirement.

Access to healthy, affordable food is another example of a firm principle that needs to be applied in various ways. Few would suggest that we should all eat the same, or that everyone should be able to afford a daily helping of caviar. Nor can a free society insist that everyone has a healthy diet. If some people choose to eat too many fried chips and cream buns, and too few lentils and grapefruits, too bad. Equality of access to healthy, affordable food means something different. In fact it means two things: first, that incomes should be high enough (and/or food prices low enough) for everyone to be able to afford a healthy diet; secondly, that shops that sell good-value, healthy food should be readily accessible to all. Too many inner-city households, especially single-parent families, live in 'food deserts'. Supermarkets and good greengrocers are beyond easy reach to those without cars; local corner stores charge high prices and sell little that is fresh and in good condition. For people living in food deserts, equality of access is partly about income and partly about the nature of our retail system. Some means of coaxing Tesco and Sainsbury to set up small 'metro' supermarkets in poor housing estates might help as much as an increase in social security benefits to achieve equality of access to healthy, affordable food.

* * *

Advocates of equality of outcome have a ready response to this argument. If incomes were distributed more evenly, there would be no food deserts, and no information under-class. Retail chains avoid poor areas precisely because they are poor: disposable income is too low to generate sufficient sales to make a profit. If the poor had more money, they could afford to join the IT revolution.

There is clearly some truth in this. Poverty is one of the biggest causes of inequality of access. It is inconceivable that equality of access can be achieved without a significant increase in the incomes of the poorest households. The argument, rather, is that poverty is not the only problem, nor higher state benefits the only answer. Some poor people have easy access to supermarkets; some less-poor people do not. If an information under-class does develop, it will include some less-poor people (especially older men and women who are terrified by computers); many younger people will know their way around the information superhighway, even if they have little money. True equality of access takes account of such points; equality of outcome does not.

Likewise – indeed, even more so – with health care. Most people depend on the National Health Service. Its quality affects almost every family. Does it provide everyone who needs it with prompt and appropriate treatment? Or are there groups who have worse access than others – the inarticulate, the elderly, residents of the wrong region or the wrong part of town? More subtly, does the (probably inevitable) concentration of the most modern, high-technology facilities into fewer, larger hospitals, give car-owners an advantage over less mobile citizens? Many of the problems caused by the closure of smaller, older hospitals relate to the fact that people who used to live only a walk or short bus-ride away, now find it hard to reach newer hospitals either for outpatient treatment or to visit friends and relations unless the local transport system is improved (new bus services and/or subsidised fares?). All these issues have clear consequences for equality of access, but little obvious connection with equality of outcome as it is normally defined.

* * *

Besides, what precisely does equality of outcome mean? Imagine two countries, Dispersia and Conformia. They have identical economies, and differ only in the range of incomes. Incomes in Dispersia range evenly from 10,000 to 40,000 groats a year – not just across the working population as a whole, but among men and women, and among white and non-white workers. Differences in income flow purely from differences in skill and experience. In Conformia things are arranged differently. All white men earn 30,000 groats a year; all white women earn 27,000 groats a year; the annual income of all non-white men is 23,000 groats, and of all non-white women 20,000.

Conformia boasts the more equal society in terms of equality-of-outcome; and, technically, it is right to do so. Every worker earns within 5,000 groats, or 20 per cent, of the mean, while incomes in Dispersia range 15,000 groats, or 60 per cent, either side of the mean. Most advocates of 'equality', however, would surely recoil from proclaiming Conformia as the more attractive society. Racial and gender discrimination are particular evils. Even people who want to turn each society into a giant kibbutz and give everyone exactly the same income would, I suspect, condemn Conformia more than Dispersia.

Apply the principle of equality of access, on the other hand, and Dispersia is obviously the preferable society. Conformia's discrimination against women and non-whites clearly violates the principle of equality of access to the labour market, even though

Dispersia has the wider gap between rich and poor. Incomes in Dispersia depend on effort and/or desert. They do not violate the principle of equality of access – provided that the disparity of incomes does not lead to violations of the principle in other areas, such as access to healthy food and reasonable housing. (Dispersia is also preferable to supporters of equality of opportunity; but this has other defects: see below.)

Back in the real world, assessments of inequality-of-outcome are far more complex, but they frequently raise similar issues. For one thing, Britain's labour market is tilted in favour of white men and against women and against black and Asian workers. The process is more subtle and less complete than in Conformia, but it still persists.

More difficult is the issue of low pay. Without generous family benefits, £4 an hour is a poverty wage for a family's bread-winner, but can be attractive for a teenager working in a fast-food restaurant and living at home, or for a family's second-earner, working part-time. Any crude statistical table that fails to differentiate these forms of low pay is apt to provide a misleading picture of the scale and impact of income inequality.

* * *

Those who claim to advocate equality of outcome seldom address such matters with any rigour. The reason is that they seldom define what they mean: absolute equality, in which everyone has an identical income, or something else. Advocates of pure equality are rare. More common are those who want greater equality, but who do not specify a desired end state. They do not say that Britain should become a giant kibbutz. Instead they adopt Crosland's approach, without sharing his candour about its limitations.

They argue that Britain is too unequal and that the government should increase taxes on the better-off to help those on benefit.

Roy Hattersley is currently Labour's most conspicuous proponent of this view:

> Over the years between 1979 and 1993–1994, the income of the richest 10 per cent of society increased by almost 60 per cent. At the same time, the income of the poorest ten per cent (after housing costs were taken into account) fell in real terms. Margaret Thatcher was the most redistributive Prime Minister in British history: her government took from the poor and gave to the rich. There was a time when the Labour Party promised to redress the balance. Sadly that may no longer be Labour's view, but the facts of poverty are beyond dispute. The poor are still with us and in greater numbers. (*The Guardian*, 26 July 1997)

Following Labour's decision to rewrite Clause Four of its constitution, Hattersley said he had 'hoped that a commitment to create an equal society would replace the promise of wholesale nationalisation. That hope was disappointed.'

Three weeks later, Peter Mandelson insisted in a Fabian lecture on social exclusion that Hattersley was wrong:

> In politics the acid test is what you end up achieving. I say to the doubters, judge us after ten years in office. For one of the fruits of that success will be that Britain has become a more equal society. However, we will have achieved that result by many different routes, not just the redistribution of cash from rich to poor, which others choose as their own limited vision of egalitarianism.

Mandelson announced the establishment of a special unit in the Cabinet Office to 'make recommendations for changes in policies, programmes and machinery effectively to tackle social exclusion.

Hattersley responded 48 hours later:

No one who has criticised the Government's poverty programme has ever suggested that income redistribution is in itself enough. Of course the causes of poverty have to be addressed. But while the long-term remedies are working through, thousands of families – some of whom can never benefit from the Welfare to Work programme – are living below the poverty line. No minister has provided an explanation of why they are not offered immediate help. (*The Times*, 16 August 1997)

Many on the left and centre–left would agree with the force of Hattersley's description of the Tory record, and with his advocacy of immediate action to fight poverty. The point, however, is that one may support his analysis and his proposals without adopting his view of equality. There is no need to believe in equality *per se* in order to wish for a whole raft of measures – ranging from more generous state benefits to better training and job opportunities – to help the poor. The scale of their plight is justification enough.

The fundamental question is this. Is greater equality an end in itself, or a means to an end? Those who believe in greater equality for its own sake oppose the acquisition of personal wealth, and want the rich to be taxed heavily, regardless of whether such acquisition does any practical harm, or punitive taxes any practical good. Those who regard greater equality as a means, not an end, take a more pragmatic view. Does an assault on the rich really help the poor?

Hattersley's *Guardian* and *Times* articles are couched in the language of egalitarianism for its own sake: the central purpose of Tony Blair's government should be 'to create an equal society'. But the specific arguments he presents are instrumental. He wants more equality in order to help the poor. He does not say whether the creation of 'an equal society' would involve stripping Richard Branson and David Sainsbury of their wealth. His rhetoric suggests that he does, but his specific proposals omit any such measure. Indeed, remove the rhetoric, and the Hattersley–Mandelson dispute turns into a disagreement about policies, not visions: about means, not ends. Hattersley wants tougher, more urgent action to end poverty; he thinks a more redistributive tax and benefits system could help the process. Mandelson doubts this and thinks a different kind of approach is needed. (Perhaps this point should be depersonalised. David Blunkett signalled Labour's new approach in a speech in February 1998 when he said:

> The truth is that any government entering the 21st century cannot hope to create a more equal or egalitarian society simply by taking from one group of people and redistributing it to others, as envisaged when the rich were very rich and the poor made up the rest. Mandelson was echoing the views of the government as a whole.

To depict the dispute between these two approaches as being about means rather than ends is not to belittle it. Most of the toughest political choices concern means more than ends. At the same time, we need to recognise that both sides have been reluctant to define the ends they seek; that is, neither has described its guiding vision. Hattersley advocates 'an equal society', Blunkett 'a more equal society'; but neither states what 'equal' fundamentally means.

The principles of equality of access would help to clarify this argument. They offer a set of clear ambitions for the left and centre–left. They also prompt a series of testing questions. How far are the victims of poverty and social exclusion simply short of money – and how far are they denied adequate access to the 'membership rights' of citizenship by other obstacles in their path? In as far as money is the problem, what is the best way to alleviate poverty? In as far as money is not the immediate problem, what measures should be taken? Equality of access does not merely shift the debate: it also provides different criteria of how to judge the attainment of an 'equal' (Hattersley) or 'more equal' (Blunkett) society. A simple indicator – showing, say, that the real incomes of the poorest 10 per cent have risen relative to the national median – would not be enough. Equality of access demands that the victims of inequality find it easier to live in decent housing, buy healthy food, secure better education for their children, obtain good health care and walk in safety at night round their neighbourhood.

* * *

What about equality of opportunity? This is the concept that ministers have tended to use to underpin their alternative to Hattersley. According to Gordon Brown, 'the essence of equality is equality of opportunity' (John Smith Memorial Lecture, 19 April 1996). A few weeks later he told me:

> The search for equalities of outcome, and even to talk as if that is the aim of the Labour Party, has led us up the wrong roads. The pursuit of equality of outcome is someone else's nightmare about socialism rather than a genuine socialist dream. I would prefer to look at equality in terms of opportunities for all. (*Analysis*, BBC Radio 4, 18 July 1996)

According to the conventional view of equality of opportunity, what matters is that everyone has an equal chance to succeed in life. Nobody should be disadvantaged at the outset because they are poor, black, female or come from a broken home. In its normal use, equality of opportunity is mainly deemed to be about education, together with measures to combat discrimination. (Hence the assertion in recruitment advertisements that 'we are an equal opportunities employer.')

Few would deny that 'equality of opportunity' has provided a useful framework for progressive policies over the years. However, as with equality of outcome, it has defied attempts to produce a full, agreed definition. It has also had trouble dealing with one acute dilemma that could arise in a society in which equality of opportunity exists. Would we be content for young adults, having been given their equal opportunities, to take their chances in the world of work and let chance and the market decide who succeeds and who fails, or does 'equality of opportunity' imply a continuing obligation on the part of life's winners to help life's losers – or is there a point at which social obligation ends and individual responsibility takes over?

Crosland was surely right when he argued that

> Equality of opportunity and social mobility, though they lead to the most admirable distribution of intelligence, are not enough. They need to be ... combined with other measures to equalise the distribution of rewards and privileges so as to diminish the degree of class stratification, the injustice of large inequalities, and the collective discontents which come from too great a dispersion of rewards.
> (*The Future of Socialism*, Chapter 8, section V)

There is a further problem with equality of opportunity. Four decades ago Michael Young – social innovator, author of Labour's 1945 manifesto, and founder of the Open University – coined the word 'meritocracy'. These days it is widely used as a positive description of an equality-of-opportunity society, where people succeed on merit, rather than according to family circumstance. What is often forgotten is that Young's book, *The Rise of the Meritocracy*, was a polemic that warned *against* the conventional view of equality of opportunity. He predicted that a truly meritocratic society would be harsh and unpleasant, in which the poor would be stigmatised more than ever (because their failure would be their own fault, not that of the social order) while the successful would become an even more arrogant and narrow-minded elite ('we have won in a fair race: what obligation do we have to those who have stumbled?').

When I interviewed Young separately for the same Radio Four Analysis programme as Gordon Brown, I asked him whether he stood by what he wrote in the 1950s. Young replied:

> I thought equality of opportunity, the way it was thought of and the way it is still thought of, was a baneful thing. I wasn't in favour of it and I'm not now either. I saw the meritocracy as becoming less and less concerned with the main body of people, establishing a sort of culture of their own, an elite culture with a good deal of arrogance in it. These things have largely happened. (*Analysis*, BBC Radio 4, 18 July 1996)

Not everyone will agree with the premise of that answer: that equality of opportunity now exists. The better-paid professions still recruit disproportionately from the families of professional households; unskilled workers and the long-term unemployed are still to be found largely among the children of unskilled and unemployed parents. In a truly meritocratic society, neither would happen. Perhaps we now have the worst of both worlds: the disadvantages of meritocracy that Young predicted, without its advantages – an end to the biases against working-class children, and an economy that makes more efficient use of the talents of its people.

Equality of access offers a solution to this problem. It is rooted in the continuing, common humanity that all citizens should share, and recognise in each other. Where equality of opportunity is apt to create meritworthy sheep and merit-challenged goats, and to provide some justification for the arrogance of the former towards the latter, equality of access seeks to avoid such consequences. Of course, no social design can prevent tensions, differences or prejudices; but at least we should try to devise an approach to equality that sets out to limit rather than exacerbate such traits.

We should note, however, that in his radio interview, Young took care to speak of 'the way it [equality of opportunity] was thought of and the way it is still thought of'. Are there other definitions? In his John Smith Memorial Lecture, Gordon Brown argued that 'equality of opportunity should not be a one-off, pass–fail, life-defining event but a continuing opportunity for everyone to have the chance to realise their potential to the full... Making equality of opportunity count means, first, ensuring lifelong equality of opportunity – not one but many opportunities.'

As with so many features of the debate about equality, the problem with 'lifelong equality of opportunity' lies not so much with the sentiment that inspires it, or with the specific policy prescriptions that flow from it, as with the rigour of the term. Opportunities are there to be seized or spurned. Success at one stage in life generally opens up wider and better opportunities at the next. 'Lifelong equality of opportunity' does not remove this manifest inequality; nor does it remove the dangers of an arrogant meritocracy.

* * *

Equality of access seeks to avoid the weaknesses of both equality of opportunity and equality of outcome. It sets a wide series of challenges to politicians who call themselves progressive; indeed, there are few areas of public policy that 'equality of access' does not touch. At the same time, it avoids ideological rigidity. It does not demand a particular form of economic organisation, or ownership of industry, or tax regime; it does not prescribe a particular, maximum range of incomes; nor does it say that wealth is bad. Rather, it invites those, inside and outside government, who design policies for the economy and social security, industry and education, the police and the health service, transport and housing, to measure the impact of their plans against equality of access criteria.

Equality of access sets challenges not only to policymakers but also to the operation of market forces. Nothing proposed here challenges the basic principles of flexible and efficient capital and labour markets, or the use of incentives. What is proposed is that the consequences of market forces need to be monitored: if and where they violate the objective of equality of access, then action should be taken to rectify matters. Such action might take various forms: wholly voluntary; response to consumer pressure; response to government concern; legal regulation; subsidies; tax changes – or some mixture of these. Solving the problem of 'food deserts' or improving bus services to large hospitals are examples of where market forces need a firm nudge.

Equality of access also provides a fresh framework for tackling social exclusion. That the poor need more money; that their plight has got worse over the past 20 years; that welfare benefits are often inadequate; all these things are beyond doubt. To that extent, it is hard to dispute Hattersley's analysis. The issue is not the description we provide of a dysfunctional society, but the vision we offer of a healthy one. The argument here is that equality of access could provide a large part of that vision: it is more rigorous than equality of outcome, and more complete than equality of opportunity. And one reason is that equality of access is multi-dimensional, concerned not just with money but with the full range of matters that determine whether people can enjoy the full fruits of citizenship.

In recent years Britain's left and centre–left have undergone a remarkable change. Under Tony Blair, Labour's ideology, constitution and policies have been transformed. Under John Monks, the trade union movement has begun to modernise its outlook and seek more constructive engagement with the business community. Under Paddy Ashdown, the Liberal Democrats have abandoned their traditional stance of equidistance between the two main parties and moved closer to Labour. All are committed to 'the project': a term that is vague, and sometimes employed ironically, but which seeks to convey the notion of progress towards some kind of better, fairer and more inclusive society.

Equality of access is a vision that could help to define 'the project'. It sets many challenges to the government; it demands radical policies in many areas; it generates a series of yardsticks by which the success or failure of Tony Blair and his ministers can be judged. And it would provide a clear answer to the question: does New Labour believe in equality?

13 The Arts of Life: Crosland's Culture*
Philip Dodd

'The words of the dead are modified in the guts of the living': to read Anthony Crosland's *The Future of Socialism*, in Blair's Britain, is to recognise the justice of Auden's words on the death of W.B. Yeats. It is uncanny how easy it is to read parts of Crosland's classic book as a commentary on New Labour's project. At times it seems he is simply Our Man in the 1950s, conjugating arguments and debates that are still unresolved. This is of course not to pretend that there are not major differences between now and then. *The Future of Socialism* was first a matter of very urgent debate within the Labour Party in the second half of the 1950s, a time when the Party had been out of power for some years; when the UK was overwhelmingly working class, at least in numerical terms (72% as late as 1951); when the Cold War was at its height, with the brutal suppression of the Hungarian uprising; and when Britain was trying (and failing) to negotiate a post-colonial identity, in the aftermath of the Suez débâcle.

But interesting arguments have a way of escaping their moment of inception and taking flight in different circumstances. If Anthony Crosland is not at the shoulder of Anthony Giddens, as he forges the identity of a Third Way politics, a *via media* between liberal market capitalism and an exhausted, and maybe terminally exhausted socialism, it is difficult to know who is. Indeed Giddens may be the Crosland of the

---
* Written for this volume.

1990s. In other ways too, Crosland's words seems alive and well. As he was one of the architects of the initial failed attempt to abolish Clause Four, it is odd that his name was so rarely invoked when the Labour Party did finally relinquish its commitment to state nationalisation, almost 40 years later. Equally, as Labour tries to modernise Britain and looks for models abroad, navigating between its traditional allegiance to the USA and an increasingly important relationship with Europe, Crosland offers a model of an earlier attempt to do so. It is even the case that the Prime Minister has been subject to the criticism that plagued Crosland, that he is in thrall to the USA, with its particular model of modernisation.

But above all, what makes Crosland our man in the 1950s is the last few pages of *The Future of Socialism*, 'Liberty and Gaiety in Private Life; The Need for a Reaction Against the Fabian Tradition', which briefly raise questions about the role of culture and of the arts in politics and national life. On the whole it simply wasn't done in the 1950s for avowedly political figures to raise such questions. Or, if they did so, it was either in the context of the Cold War, or in the belief that they were matters that could be tackled only after the 'real' matters of politics were resolved. To read these pages now, with their grasp of culture as a both a set of artistic activities and as the substance of civil society, is to see afresh maybe the most complex part of the Blair project, its concern with culture and creativity, a concern that found one formulation when Chris Smith, the Minister for Culture, Media and Sport, published his *Creative Britain* pamphlet in the Spring of 1998, not with HMSO, but with that fashionable publishing house, Faber. The words of the dead are indeed modified in the guts of the living. Here is one passage from 'Liberty and Gaiety in Private Life':

We need not only higher exports and old-age pensions, but more open-air cafes...later closing hours for public houses, more local repertory theatres... more pleasure gardens on the Battersea model... better designs for furniture and pottery and women's clothes...better designed street lamps ... The enemy in all this will often be in unexpected guise; it is not only dark Satanic things and people that now bar the road to the new Jerusalem, but also, if not mainly, hygienic, respectable, virtuous things and people, lacking only in grace and gaiety.

All these things are necessary if Britain is to become a 'more colourful and civilised country to live in'. Such convictions clearly seem to speak directly to this government's interest in culture. For instance, whatever the final achievements of the Millennium Dome, no one could be in doubt that Crosland, in the light of these words from *The Future of Socialism* would have supported the principle of the project. He would have seen that the Dome has the potential to be (a gigantic) pleasure garden. More importantly, he would have seen that a new Britain needs forms of national celebration other than those Royal occasions – from coronations through Royal weddings to the Jubilee – that have been the sanctioned forms of public celebration in Britain throughout the postwar period. He would have seen that the Dome has the chance to be a post-Royal public experience (rather than an event staged on our behalf by them); and that such a cultural project is not a distraction from 'real politics' but a constituent part of any ambitious political project that wants to modernise Britain.

But to understand fully the importance of those last pages of *The Future of Socialism*, both to the 1950s and the 1990s, it is necessary to understand just how mean old Labour's attitude to culture and pleasure has been (and in some parts continues to be). Although the 1950s is remembered in terms of key political events in the Cold War it is was also a moment of immense cultural change – indeed the 1960s might be said to have begun earlier than orthodox accounts allow, perhaps in the mid-fifties, the moment when Mary Quant first opened a boutique on the Kings Road in Chelsea. It was to that world of cultural change that *The Future of Socialism* was directed and in which it was subsequently read – a world where rationing was finally abolished and which had seen the inauguration of commercial television, not only challenging the monopoly of the BBC, but also bringing advertising of consumer goods into the home. If in 1951 there had been 2.5 million television sets in Britain by 1964, there were to be 13 million. It was also a Britain where American culture was becoming more and more dominant – one can see as much in the NUT–Communist Party moral panic over American comics corrupting British children, in the arrival of American rock'n'roll, and tours such as those of Bill Haley in 1957. Above all, it was a world where post-colonial peoples were coming to settle in Britain, with their potential to transform British culture.

Not the least part of Crosland's distinctiveness at that time was his openness to cultural change, not a quality easily located elsewhere in a party, which on the whole was always more comfortable with precedent rather than newness (Blair's interest in novelty makes the PM himself a novelty in Labour culture). As Crosland recognised, there was a strand within Labour culture – a strand made up of 'hygienic, respectable, virtuous people', which drew on the Fabian tradition of the Webbs and which preferred 'hard work, self-discipline, efficiency and abstinence' rather than the pleasures of the emergent consumer culture. It is always noticeable that it is those who have chosen to relinquish such consumer pleasures who are the most vocal in railing against the acquisition of such pleasures by the kinds of people who have never before had the opportunity to experience them. With the enormous condescension of posterity, it is easy to make fun of the judgements of the past, but what else can one do when one reads Richard Crossman in the 1950s pointing to 'the luxuries, gadgets, entertainments and packaged foodstuffs which so many workers enjoy in our Affluent Societies' as ' irrelevant and even vulgar and immoral'. Maybe the syntax is careless, but there is a sense in which Crossman seems to equate domestic appliances and entertainment with vulgarity and immorality. How could packaged foodstuffs (and Crossman was no closet green politician) be immoral? Unfortunately, this is the authentic view of one dominant strand of Labour thinking about popular pleasures and popular culture: remember Tony Benn's disgust at the vulgar decoration of recently purchased council houses? It is this kind of thinking that drove the Arts Council, an important postwar initiative, to separate out the fine art 'sheep', which it would nourish and sustain, from the popular culture 'goats' which could survive on their own wits, ensuring that British film, as much as British popular music, not to mention fashion and design, would not be given Arts Council support for decades. It is not the least of this current government's virtues that it has refused these traditional distinctions between high and low, fine and applied arts, and has supported design and fashion, as much as the more traditional arts. In this sense the government seems to be taking its lead from the injunctions of Crosland who moves without trouble or anxiety across art and cultural forms (from paintings to eating places, from repertory theatres to better designed street lamps); and shows a confidence in popular judgements. He even speaks up for the sartorial elegance of the Teddy Boys and notes how they are steeped 'in what is now becoming a genuine popular culture among the young – the study of jazz'. On the other hand, Richard Crossman speaks for the opposite tendency. He believes he knows (*droit de seigneur?*) what is to be counted as art and what is entertainment, without any idea that the categories are historically variable. To take a simple example: my father grew up in a mining community, enthralled by John Wayne's cowboy movies, which are now routinely taught in higher education as John Ford westerns, rightly held up as one of the great achievements of American culture. Or take an example from British culture. Dickens' novels may have been written for a popular audience and consumed as entertainment, but they have come to be recognised as amongst the best of English literature. Walter Savage Landor who wrote Latin poems during the same period, as art, distancing himself from entertainment, is now relegated to the realm of Casaubon-like arcane scholarship.

It is only with an understanding of how defensive and frightened of cultural novelty were the bright young things of the 1950s' Labour Party, that it is possible to measure Crosland's audacity and perspicuity. And of course the defensiveness and anxiety have not altogether gone away. When David Blunkett, the current Minister for Education, rails against the decision of the British Council to send Mark Ravenshill's play, *Shopping and F****, overseas as an example of British contemporary culture, not on the grounds that it is a poor play (which it is), but rather on the grounds that it is immoral – then one understands why Crosland's admonitions are still pertinent.

On the whole Labour has always preferred its supporters – as its name suggests – to be heroically labouring, rather than frivolously playing. Just think of Orwell's *The Road to Wigan Pier* with its hymn to coal-mining and its comparison of the well-made bodies of the coal-miners to those of guardsman. Orwell is only the most prominent example of those for whom Labour is about Men at Work (and as in Orwell's case it was almost always men). Maybe it is that enthralment to Men at Work that has made Labour so uneasy when its supporters choose rather to enjoy themselves. Just think of Richard Hoggart's *Uses of Literacy*, published only two years after *The Future of Socialism*, with its loathing of new forms of leisure – the American 'candy floss' world of milk bars and juke boxes. Hoggart is much happier in the insulated interior world of Hunslett, Leeds, with its tight, closely-knit, working-class communities. There's a Hoggartian quality to one of the best current Labour historians – Ross McKibbon's book *Classes and Culture: England 1918–1951*, with its warm nostalgic prose in praise of pigeon fancying and the works outing. In the context of such determined insularity and nostalgia, Crosland's untroubled recognition that rising incomes were already making holidays abroad a possibility for the many and not only the few makes him sound not only clear-sighted about future leisure patterns, but also positively utopian about the capacities of ordinary people to embrace novel experiences and make reasonable cultural judgements.

Perhaps the one strand of socialist thinking that came closest to Crosland's is the one that took him seriously as an adversary: the New Left of the 1950s. This intellectual movement, that would dominate cultural thought, particularly in the academy, right up to the nineties, had as its key players Raymond Williams, E.P. Thompson and Stuart Hall. In a recent essay on the emergence of the New Left, Stuart Hall mentions that in 1956, as his summer reading, and as a prelude to writing a book on the new contours of cultural change in 'Contemporary Capitalism', he consumed a number of key texts which he itemises. At the head of the list is Crosland's *The Future of Socialism*. There may be many important things that separated Crosland and the New Left: for instance, Crosland's acceptance of an Atlanticist world view; the New Left's sense of culture as at least in part the continuation of political struggle by other means. But what binds them together – and separates them both out from the dominant Labour thinking in the 1950s – is their conviction that what counted as politics was thin and mean. Both saw that man and woman couldn't live by elections, political meetings and economic indicators alone; that economic well-being, plus welfare, wasn't an adequate political vision and did not provide the conditions for an adequate individual or national life. In this context it is telling that William Morris was the common touchstone of both Crosland and the New Left (E.P. Thompson's biography of Morris was published in 1953). Both saw him as interrogating received definition of politics and finding them wanting; both saw him as offering a rich and complex account of what might count as the good life.

It may be that 1968 is commonly and rightly credited with the remaking of politics as an inclusive rather than exclusive activity, one that accommodates the concerns of social and cultural life, but if so, then *The Future of Socialism* (as well as the New Left) laid some of the ground for that remaking. Insofar as New Labour's project is at least as much about modernising civil society, as much as political structures, then it too owes its debt to those anti-Fabian forces of the 1950s, Crosland included. Certainly Crosland's commitment, in 1956, to a whole host of reforms in civil society is extremely impressive, whether to the liberalisation of divorce laws or the repeal of laws against homosexuality, whether the removal of 'prehistoric (and flagrantly unfair) abortion laws' or the abandonment of the 'illiterate censorship of books and plays'. To read his intolerance of such restrictions, his belief that in the blood of socialists there should always run 'a trace of the anarchist and the libertarian' is to recognise the correspondence between Crosland's own beliefs and at least some of those of the current Labour government, including its determination to equalise the age of consent for gays and heterosexuals despite the resistence of the still unreformed House of Lords. But it is also to find a measure against which to judge some of the current Labour administration's populist authoritarianism. If one of this Government's key projects is to re-regulate moral life after the 1980s' deregulation, then it could learn from the open non-puritanical stance of Crosland's *The Future of Socialism* and fight shy of Labour's historical tendency to show, in Crosland's words, 'more orthodoxy than a bench of bishops'.

Generally, Crosland's confidence in the judgement of the people – his willingness to trust them – is one of the driving forces behind much of *The Future of Socialism*; and this is particularly the case whenever culture is discussed. The whole book has its face set against those who assume, to use today's phrase, that 'dumbing down' is an inevitable consequence of increased access to cultural resources – whether those of higher education or of the Royal Opera House. Chris Smith's mantra, 'For the Many not the Few', might have been developed out of a reading of *The Future of Socialism* and is certainly unnerving professional administrators in the arts. And so it should. They have wielded considerable power and from the immediate postwar period have stood as gatekeepers, sifting what was and was not to be supported and thus available. Of course, changes in technology have partly thrown that power into doubt. For instance, video now allows people to programme their own cinema season (courtesy of the market), watching in their home Hollywood films and 'world cinema', where once they would have had such films institutionally segregated and programmed for them (the Odeon chain for Hollywood; the art-house circuit for foreign films). But equally the power of the gatekeepers is diluted because the present government is calling to democratic account those cultural institutions given public subsidy, asking questions that ought to have been asked years ago. To listen to some of those opposing such accounting is to hear again the strains of those whom Crosland attacked – and who claimed 'that equality and culture are mutually antagonistic'. They are not. After all, the history of culture in Britain is partly the history of the struggle to gain access to that culture. As early as the eighteenth century and the development of the novel, there were claims that access to the novel by women was weakening their attachment to their traditional responsibilities. *Plus ca change*.

Above all, what makes Crosland Our Man in the 1950s is his grasp that culture would become more and more important, both as an economic activity and as a chosen pursuit in an increasingly leisured society. It is that perception that drives some of the current Labour administration's most important, if contentious, policies. Re-branding Britain and Cool Britannia are at one level attempts to offer back to the British people, and to the outside world, an image of Britain far removed from that of warm beer and village greens, in order to facilitate the modernisation of Britain. But at another level, Labour's fascination with culture is a recognition that Britain needs to leave behind its vision of itself as an industrial society and understand that the new information society will be built, to use the words of Charles Leadbetter *The New Statesman* (8 May 1998), on 'intangible assets such as knowledge, ideas and creativity' as much as on 'financial and physical capital'. In this scenario, culture is both the model for economic activity and its driving force. While it would be disingenuous to say that, in 1956, Crosland had grasped all this, it would be equally unfair not to recognise that Crosland got nearer than any other thinker to understanding what was happening. For a man remembered as an important Labour politician and as a political thinker, it would be a splendid irony if his substantial bequest to us is the recognition that culture will now matter more than either traditional politics or traditional economics.

14 Crosland, European Social Democracy and New Labour*
Daniel Wincott

A full evaluation of Anthony Crosland as a theorist and practitioner of Social Democracy requires that he be placed in a broader context than is usually the case. In particular, his contribution has to be analysed in relation to both British and other European Social Democratic traditions and experiences. A central argument of this chapter is that Crosland is the nearest thing to a radical 'European-style' Social Democrat that English politics has produced in the postwar period. Such a perspective marks Crosland out as more radical than many of his revisionist colleagues – a potentially controversial position in both the British and the wider European debates. Many of the strengths of his position reflect the mixture of pragmatism and a continuing radicalism which is, I think, characteristic of the most successful of Europe's Social Democratic Parties. In general, Social Democratic theorists working in the European tradition have criticised Crosland for a failure to be sufficiently radical (Esping-Andersen, 1985, 1990; see also Stephens, 1979; King, 1987; Hutton, 1996). While there is something in these criticisms, I want to defend Crosland from them, to some extent. They run a risk of purism – 'ideal' elements are taken out of the political context in which they developed and 'applied' in

---

* Written for this volume.

another, quite distinct setting. Crosland's work was at least as much an intervention in British politics, particularly the politics of the Labour Party, as it was a contribution to the theory of Social Democracy. Radical Social Democratic (or Democratic Socialist) critics of Crosland pay too little attention to the domestic context within and against which Crosland was working. The idiosyncrasies of 'Social Democracy' in Britain are likely to be increasingly recognised over the next few years, in my view. The 'weaknesses' which radical Social Democrats detect in Crosland's work may be the product of these oddities of Labour Party politics.

THE EUROPEAN INFLUENCE ON CROSLAND'S SOCIAL DEMOCRACY

Considering Crosland's vision of Social Democracy in the context of the European experience throws up something of a paradox. On the one hand, Crosland drew significantly on aspects of European Social Democracy. Indeed, I believe that European Social Democracy was at least as important an influence on Crosland as the US academy and politics. The Swedish SAP – and, after *Bad Godesberg* (1959 see below), the German SPD – were particularly important influences on him. On the other hand, many theorists of European Social Democracy are roundly critical of Crosland, apparently identifying his revisionism with a lack of radicalism. The influence on Crosland of the European experience was especially important in two areas: the possibilities of taxation/public expenditure and the role of nationalisation. On the first of these issues Crosland regularly pointed to levels of public expenditure elsewhere in order to undercut claims that levels in the UK were unsustainable (see Crosland, 1956, p. 407, 1962, p. 13). It is interesting to note that while the proportion of national income taken by the British State was comparatively high in the early 1950s, in the course of that decade it grew much more rapidly elsewhere in Europe than it did in Britain – Crosland made the argument that UK public expenditure was relatively low much more forcefully in *The Conservative Enemy* than he had done in *The Future of Socialism*.

More significant for the argument developed here, examples drawn from the experience of Social Democracy elsewhere in Europe were a key to Crosland's attempt to dislodge the commitment to nationalisation from its central position in Labour Party ideology. Of course, European Social Democracy was not the only source on which Crosland drew for the development of these ideas: American sociology, economics and organisational theory had made its mark on him – as scattered references to Mayo, Merton and Veblen in *The Future of Socialism* indicate. For Crosland Scandinavia 'prove[d] that wholesale nationalisation is not a necessary condition of greater equality' or Social Democratic success (Crosland 1956: p. 485). Within three years of the publication of *The Future of Socialism* the German SPD's adoption of the *Bad Godesberg* programme, in which public ownership was repudiated as a central policy objective provided Crosland with further ammunition for the fight to 'de-centre' nationalisation (Crosland alluded to these changes in *The Conservative Enemy*, 1962, pp. 128–9, and discussed them in *Social Democracy in Europe* 1975, pp. 10–11). The Labour Party's concern with nationalisation was viewed by Crosland as 'unique' amongst European socialist parties (Crosland, 1975, p. 10). For Crosland, much of the energy expended on this issue was wasted, reflecting 'a narrow and insular conservatism which in turn stems largely from basic weaknesses in our social class structures' (Crosland 1975, p. 11). However, it may be the case that in looking to the experience of European Social Democracy to justify the sidelining of nationalisation, Crosland under-estimated the importance of other strategies adopted in order to divide power and control from ownership. I will return to this question shortly – for now, it is sufficient to note that any misjudgement he may have made on this question was probably owed to his reading of American sociology and organisation theory, where influential theorists suggested that modern management and organisation had already effectively separated ownership from control.

A (EUROPEAN) SOCIAL DEMOCRATIC CRITIQUE OF CROSLAND?

Turning to the critique of Crosland, it revolves around two main issues: economic growth and the significance of 'ownership'. On the first of these issues, as King (1987, pp. 61–2) argues, economic growth was absolutely central to Crosland's vision. It was only if economic growth could be sustained that Crosland believed significant redistribution could be achieved. Moreover, his adherence to Keynesian ideas meant that for a good part of his political and intellectual life Crosland believed that economic growth ought not to be especially difficult to achieve. He remained committed to this vision even when environmentalists began to question the normative desirability of growth and economic conditions made its attainment seem more problematic (see Lipsey 1981, pp. 26–33, for a discussion). However, after *The Future of Socialism* Crosland became more aware of the difficulty of promoting economic growth (see Crosland, 1974, p: 73)

The second question – that of the significance of ownership in the economy – is even more important than the first, given Crosland's view of nationalisation. Essentially the argument is that Crosland underestimated the extent to which ownership and control remained interconnected in the postwar world. As a consequence, the argument runs, he was able to focus on the big levers of power – the overall steering of the economy and the broad impact of public expenditure on the welfare state. Gøsta Esping-Andersen, one of today's leading analysts of European Social Democracy, called this the 'Keynes plus Beveridge' policy (1985, p 24). On his view, Crosland under-estimated the significance of the *strategy* Swedish Social Democrats devised for wresting control away from ownership, because he *assumed* that ownership no longer coincided with control (Esping-Andersen, 1985, p. 23; see also Stephens, 1979, pp. 69–72). Immediate social reforms provided the pre-condition for a further economic democratisation according to Swedish Social Democrats. Moreover, the detailed content of social policy was usually constructed so as to help transform power relations in the workplace.

THE IMPORTANCE OF CONTEXT

While there is some truth in the radical European critique, I believe that Crosland can be largely defended against it on two grounds. First, it seems to me that the critique ignores his long interest in industrial democracy and the cooperative movement. Now, it is true to say that, particularly in the 1950s and 1960s Crosland was sceptical about the involvement of workers in the higher management of enterprises – instead regarding the appropriate forum for workers (the union) as being essentially independent of management. Nevertheless, from *The Future of Socialism* onwards, industrial democracy was an important theme in his work. Moreover, in the

1970s he changed position on the issue, to some extent (see Crosland, 1974, pp. 49–53; Radice, 1981, pp. 119–21).

Second, and perhaps more important, the radical European critique has something of a purist feel about it. It pays little attention to the fact that Crosland's arguments were neither purely abstract nor academic theories: they were contributions to – interventions in – the public debate in Britain. This neglect of context is not characteristic of recent European Social Democratic theory. On the contrary, Esping-Andersen is closely associated with analysis which examines the variety of forms of state structure in capitalist democracies, an analysis which places particular emphasis on the interaction of the choices of political agents – parties, coalitions and other groups with these structures. Esping-Andersen (1990) focuses in turn on the role of political parties construction of (welfare) state structures, and the manner in which the state forms then structures the 'space' in which, and resources with which, parties pursue their strategies. An important lesson about the nature of the mixed economy ought to be drawn out of this sort of analysis (although it is only rarely). The notion that the mixed economy occupies a middle point on a continuum between the free market and socialism is misleading. 'Models' of a broadly capitalist economy exist, within which the state plays a substantial role, but which are by no means socialist or even social democratic. For example, the German state has often played a major broadly constructive role in the economy, frequently without achieving or even seeking to achieve social democratic purposes. The range of potential or viable strategies that Social Democrats could pursue clearly varies with these aspects of the context within which they find themselves.

Crosland himself at times may have fallen prey to the notion that the nature and extent of state involvement in the economy in Western European countries took a common form and reflected Social Democratic priorities and achievements, at least outside of the UK (although outside of the European context he was remarkably sensitive to this issue – see Crosland, 1956, pp. 520–1). Breaking with this image allows us to evaluate Crosland's political thought in the intellectual context of Labour Party and wider British debates and the practical political context of the sorts of alliances and strategies open to him. In the more successful of Europe's Social Democratic Parties a *radical* revisionism came to be much more deeply rooted and widely supported than it ever was in the Labour Party. Moreover, although the Social Democrats enjoyed different strategic resources in Sweden and Germany, with the SPD generally in a weaker position that the SAP, both were in a stronger position than the Labour Party. Moreover, at least during the first 40 years after the Second World War, the SAP and the SPD seem to have made better use of the strategic space available to them than the Labour Party did. The question of the strategic location of, and resources available to, these parties cannot be separated from the question of the strategic choices they have made. Indeed, one reason for this relative strength when compared with Labour was the much more thorough-going adoption of key elements of the 'revisionist' case (particularly the jettisoning of the assumption that nationalisation was a good thing in and of itself), while retaining key elements of a gradualist and democratic radicalism.

Some theorists of European Social Democracy who are critical of Crosland's views on economic and welfare policy praise some other aspects of his analysis. Esping-Andersen, for example, is intrigued by Crosland's concern that socialism should be more 'fun' than capitalism. As Esping-Andersen points out, before Social Democrats gained access to state power, considerable energy was devoted to the consolidation of their constituency by organising clubs and leisure organisations of various sorts (Esping-Andersen, 1985, p. 24). This effort faltered as social democratic parties became political bureaucracies, partly as a consequence of the left gaining (access to) state power. However, even where they praise Crosland, the sense of the particular context within which his thought developed, is not fully present in the work of European Social Democratic theorists. In fact, Crosland's concern with fun – 'culture, beauty, leisure, and even frivolity' (1956, p. 524) was a specific reaction against certain tendencies in English Fabianism and more generally against the English class system. Crosland seems to have believed that these qualities of civilised life were 'European' characteristics, identifying as he did German 'civic enterprise in town-planning, housing and patronage of the arts and Swedish 'high cultural and aesthetic standards, a strong social conscience, and the high prestige of public activity' (Crosland, 1962, p. 27). By contrast Crosland saw Britain as a 'philistine ... insular and unimaginative country' with 'exceptionally low cultural expectations and ... extraordinary passivity in the face of squalor and discomfort' in private as well as public services (Crosland, 1962, pp. 26–7, 47). This image of other countries certainly had a romantic dimension.

Ironically, however, the sense of both the peculiarity of, and the necessity of transforming, the British class structure may have been – indeed may continue to be – a prerequisite for a wider transformation of the state, economy and society. I cannot claim that Crosland saw the issue in precisely this way, for at least two reasons. First, he appears to have believed that elements of egalitarianism in other societies, even including the USA, meant that they faced a different–and seemingly smaller–need for social and economic transformation. Second, for all that Crosland's interest in the concerns of his Grimsby constituents often outweighed his concern with the interests of NW3 (see Lipsey 1981, p. 36) there was sometimes a slightly elitist sense that he sought to raise the aspirations of wage slaves to the 'better things' enjoyed by the upper middle classes (although at times he was sensitive to the distinctiveness of the expressed desires of his constituents – see, for example, Crosland, 1974, p. 79). For example, for all its strengths comprehensive secondary education, with which Crosland was closely associated, had several flaws. Arguably, they are owed to the notion that the comprehensives could and should extend grammar school aspirations throughout the system, and a consequent neglect and under-valuing of other facets of education, particularly the more technical ones.

Nevertheless, Crosland's view of equality was more complex that its conventional equation with welfare statism would suggest. Although, arguably Crosland should be even more closely associated with the 'welfare statist' view than he is, there was more to his egalitarianism than the welfare state. It is easy to forget that socialists have not always seen social policy as means of increasing equality. Before the Second World War many socialists valued the potential of social policy to facilitate solidarity among workers, by partly insulating them from the 'whip' of the market (Esping-Andersen, 1985, p. 148). Crosland was one of the earliest theoretical proponents of 'socialism as welfare statist equality'(see the comments in Esping-Andersen, 1985, p. 148). However, Crosland's egalitarianism was also motivated by the desire to make the 'things that he himself liked and enjoyed ... available to everybody – including, specifically, to his working class constituents in Grimsby – rather than being restricted to the few' as Dick Leonard (1981, p.11) has put it. Both this aspect of his view of equality and the overall vision had their faults. Moreover, it was not clear exactly how they could be brought into being. However, the sense that a social transformation was necessary if important weaknesses in industry were to be addressed was a key element in Crosland's thought and he expected that such a transformation would alter the framework of ideas on both sides of British politics. This sense is undervalued in the critique of Crosland.

THE FUTURE: NEW LABOUR AND EUROPEAN SOCIAL DEMOCRACY

Today, any reconsideration of European traditions of Social Democracy, and Crosland's position within them, must confront the question 'what is left for the left?' In many European countries – including some of the states in which it is widely regarded as having powerful influence – Social Democracy seems to be in chaos. The Swedish 'model' is often depicted as being in full retreat, the socialist government in France is engaged in massive public expenditure cuts and even the *'modell Deutschland'* on which the SPD had a significant influence is, many argue, subject to increasing pressure. In this context if the 'peculiarities' of British politics made 'New Labour' possible then many self-defined 'Social Democrats' may welcome them. Of parties coming out of a left of centre tradition, Labour is all but unique in its electoral popularity and one of the few such parties currently displaying a sense of self-confidence. Some aspects of the 'New Labour' agenda do address long-standing institutional and cultural problems. Institutionally there is some evidence that momentum has grown up behind a major overhaul of the British State, commencing with devolution to Scotland and Wales, encompassing the return of elected government to

London as well as electoral reform, and perhaps culminating in some form of regional government for England. In addition, Tony Blair does seem to have introduced a refreshing informality between politicians and the public. This change may reflect and embody a welcome reduction of the influence of class traditions and constraints in British politics.

The pressures on European Social Democracy are often attributed to 'globalisation'. However, although a number of changes *have* occurred which increase the influence of non-state actors with something of a transnational or 'global outlook' (particularly in financial markets) the intellectual credibility of the concept of 'globalisation' is being increasingly subject to rigorous questioning (see in particular Hirst and Thompson, 1996; Wincott, 1998). The backlash against 'globalisation' suggests that the power of the forces ranged against the state, and particularly Social Democracy, has been greatly exaggerated. If this is the case, we nevertheless require an explanation for the apparent downgrading of Social Democratic ambitions – if not the dismantling of Social Democratic achievements. The possibility that 'globalisation' may have had an impact, not so much as a series of irresistible material trends, but as a cluster of *ideas*, needs consideration. The background of ideas against which Crosland developed his analysis implied that sustained, regular, economic growth was possible *and* could be combined with increasing public expenditure. These ideas played a central role in his political vision. Keynesian ideas and a rather general feeling that to a range of relevant actors it seemed legitimate for governments to pursue relatively expansionary and interventionist policies. The declining influence of these ideas, and their replacement by a more market oriented *Zeitgeist* (in combination with other changes, of course) has had a restrictive impact on Social Democrats in government, although some of these governments may have restricted their policy agendas rather more than they had to *in anticipation* of external constraints. In this context, big questions about 'The Future of Socialism' – or of Social Democracy – do need to be posed again. This chapter contributes to that massive task only indirectly, if it does so at all, by providing a re-evaluation of Crosland's political thought and practice in the mixed context of Britain and Europe.

References

Crosland, A. (1956) *The Future of Socialism* (Jonathan Cape).
Crosland, A. (1962) *The Conservative Enemy* (Jonathan Cape).
Crosland, A. (1974) *Socialism Now* (Jonathan Cape).
Crosland, A. (1975) '*Social Democracy in Europe*', Fabian Tract, 438.
Crouch, C. (1981) 'The Place of Public Expenditure in Socialist Thought', in D. Lipsey, and D. Leonard, *The Socialist Agenda: Crosland's Legacy* (Jonathan Cape).
Donaldson, Lord (1981) 'In Memoriam: II', in D. Lipsey and D. Leonard, *The Socialist Agenda: Crosland's Legacy* (Jonathan Cape).
Esping-Andersen, G. (1985) *Politics Against Markets: The Social Democratic Road to Power* (Princeton University Press).
Esping-Andersen, G. (1990) *The Three Worlds of Welfare Capitalism* (Polity).
Hirst, P. and G. Thompson (1996) *Globalization in Question* (Polity).
Hutton, W. (1996) *The State We're In* (London: Vintage).
King, D. (1987) *The New Right: Politics, Markets and Citizenship* (Macmillan).
Leonard, D. (1981) 'In Memoriam: I', in D. Lipsey and D. Leonard, *The Socialist Agenda: Crosland's Legacy* (Jonathan Cape).
Lipsey, D (1981) 'Crosland's Socialism', in D. Lipsey and D. Leonard *The Socialist Agenda: Crosland's Legacy* (Jonathan Cape).
Lipsey, D and D. Leonard (1981) *The Socialist Agenda: Crosland's Legacy* (Jonathan Cape).
Plant, R. (1981) 'Democratic Socialism and Equality', in D. Lipsey and D. Leonard, *The Socialist Agenda: Crosland's Legacy* (Jonathan Cape).
Radice, G. (1981) 'Labour and the Unions', in D. Lipsey and D. Leonard, *The Socialist Agenda: Crosland's Legacy* (Jonathan Cape).

Stephens, J. (1979) *The Transformation from Capitalism to Socialism* (Macmillan).

Wincott, D. (1998) 'Globalisation and European Integration', in C. Hay and D. Marsh (eds), *Globalisation: Critical Perspectives* (Macmillan).

15 New Labour, Old Crosland?*

Tony Wright

I only met Tony Crosland once at close quarters. It was about 1972 and I had foolishly applied to be a Rowntree 'chocolate soldier'[1] with the Labour Shadow Cabinet. The interview at the Commons, with Roy Jenkins presiding, seemed to be going rather well. Tony Crosland was slumped under a cloud of cigar smoke in the chair next to mine, his leg flopping over the side. He seemed to be feeling the effects of a hard night, looked bored by the whole proceedings – and said not a word. Until the end. Then he stirred. 'So tell us', he drawled, blowing a gentle breeze of smoke in my direction, 'how would *you* solve the problems of the British economy?' That was the moment I failed to get the job. I have always felt deeply grateful to him.

'It is surely time...to stop searching for fresh inspiration in the old orthodoxies, and thumbing over the classic texts as though they could give oracular guidance for the future.' Crosland's advice in the 1950s should be applied to his own work now. The future of socialism is not to be found in *The Future of Socialism* and it would be absurd if it was. He was grappling with his world and we have to grapple with ours. Although it has acquired a cosy sepia glow now, the intellectual and political challenges presented by that postwar world to thinkers on the left seemed every bit as daunting and intractable as the challenges of today. We need to demonstrate as much intellectual audacity and political

---

* Written for this volume.

courage in confronting our world as Tony Crosland displayed in confronting his. If we search for his enduring legacy, it is surely this.

In all kinds of ways he seems a very distant figure. In our preoccupation with globalisation, we smile wryly at the fact that the leading socialist thinker of a generation ago could preface his major work with a casual declaration that his focus was entirely domestic and would take no account of the wider world. We marvel that it was so recently that he could announce with such sweeping historical confidence of a Keynes-plus-Beveridge kind that the problems of capitalism had been solved, full employment was here to stay, poverty had been eliminated and that a quite new kind of politics (rather chillingly described as 'statism' in Crosland's contribution to *New Fabian Essays* in 1952) had been established. Issues that are central to us now – how to reform the state, how to safeguard the natural environment – either failed to interest Crosland at all or were dismissed witheringly as special pleading by the middle classes. Just as Marx, with his attachment to historical laws, was typical of a certain kind of nineteenth-century thinker, Crosland now looks like a characteristic theorist of the generation of the long postwar boom.

None of this diminishes his importance or achievement. It merely puts his thought in context. He still provides a valuable reference point for subsequent developments, as long as his own warning about biblical orthodoxies and oracular utterances is heeded. It is only necessary to recall the *Tribune* headline above its review of *The Future of Socialism* - 'Socialism? How Does He Dare Use The Word?' – to understand that context is all. Every socialist is a permanent revisionist, or should be. The revisionism of one generation is the orthodoxy of the next, requiring a new revisionism to test it against changing circumstances and keep ossification at bay. What endure are values, the fundamental benchmark against which policies and programmes are measured and developed. The importance of this distinction between ends and means was one of Crosland's insistent themes. If ends and means are confused (and this was Crosland's charge against Labour's Clause Four collectivism) then there is a category mistake. If ends and means become disconnected, though, then something even more serious results. There can be no doubt that the making of New Labour – above all, its new statement of values and its wider electoral appeal – fulfils old Croslandite ambitions. The nature of the connection between old values and new programmes raises more interesting issues.

In the ground-breaking exercise at the start of his 1956 book, Crosland set about identifying the values of socialism and from these he sifted out what he regarded as the most relevant contemporary ones. The full list had five elements: a protest against capitalist poverty and squalor, a wider concern for social welfare, a belief in equality and classlessness, a rejection of competition and embrace of cooperation, and a protest against capitalist inefficiency. In Crosland's view, the first and last items had largely lost their relevance as capitalism had been transformed, while the idea of cooperative social purpose raised too many problems. This left social welfare and social equality as the enduring socialist values with a contemporary relevance, the basis for a 'purposeful, constructive, and discriminating determination to improve an already improved society'.

We might want to put some of this rather differently now, even leaving aside Crosland's over-sanguine account of social and economic trends. In part, this is simply a matter of linguistic reshuffling: in the chorus line of ideas some are called into prominence at different times in response to changing demands. But it is also because Crosland's approach is unnecessarily confusing. The traditional socialist charge against capitalism always had two main themes, with modulations around each. One charge was that capitalism was inefficient as an economic system (producing slumps, unemployment, etc.). The other charge was that it was unjust and immoral (producing inequality, subordination, poverty, insecurity, etc.). In other words, the socialist argument has always been both empirical and moral in various combinations. If Marx's error (or one of them) was to seek to make it entirely empirical, Crosland's approach carried with it the danger of an opposite one-sidedness. The assumption that capitalism had solved its problems was more than a shift of emphasis in an ancestral dualism.

This is more than a matter of confusing passing trends with eternal truths. It undercuts a substantial part of the traditional socialist critique of capitalism. An important part of the function of socialism has been to provide such a critique of the way in which a capitalist market economy works – and then to demand that such deficiencies are remedied in the public interest. While Crosland was right to challenge a traditional argument that centred on ownership, he went much too far in accepting that capitalism had finally been domesticated. At a time when the untamed imperatives of global capital are demanding that societies and economies are reshaped in their image, Crosland can seem very distant indeed. We know that market economies have many dynamic virtues. We may even think that there are no viable alternatives available. But we also need to recognise that there are different kinds of capitalism, that markets still require a balancing public interest framework, and that global capitalism urgently needs new frameworks of regulatory stability. It is from the strand of socialist argument that Crosland – writing at a particular moment – dismissed too lightly that insight into these contemporary issues can still be derived. Yet Crosland was emphatically right, against the Marxists, to insist that it was the other strand of socialism – with its focus on core values – that the essence of the matter was to be found. Here, too, though, we find ourselves wanting to express the arguments somewhat differently today. In the less fractured world of the 1950s, he could be cavalier in his dismissal of fraternity and cooperation as socialist ideals ('indeed the trend toward 'sociability' is now so strong that we are more likely to be deprived of solitude than company'), whereas the issue of social cohesion lies at the centre of current concerns. It is not difficult to imagine the famously libertarian Crosland aghast at what he might regard as nannyist tendencies intent on telling individuals how to live their lives, but we are more inclined than he was to see socialism as a doctrine of community. There need be nothing suffocating or oppressive about this, except for those who have been reared only on the thin gruel of liberalism. As social fragmentation increases, fuelled by the forces of market individualism, it is scarcely surprising that socialism (or social-ism) has rediscovered its community credentials. It involves a recognition that society is a common enterprise, a matter of mutual social responsibility, with a reciprocity of rights and duties. If Crosland was happy to bury this aspect of the socialist tradition, we have been busily rediscovering it. It provides the indispensable foundation for a modern civic socialism.

However, it is only the foundation. The distinctive shape, distinguishing socialist from other versions of community, comes from what goes on top of it. Here Crosland offered welfare and equality. Welfare meant attending to the needs of those who had least; it was not about equality but about humanity; and for a socialist it was the first claim on expenditure. Yet even this view of welfare necessarily involved a prior belief in collective social responsibility, as Crosland tacitly acknowledged. But it was equality that was the quintessential socialist value:

> the socialist seeks a distribution of rewards, status, and privileges egalitarian enough to minimise social resentment, to secure justice between individuals, and to equalise opportunities; and he seeks to weaken the existing deep-seated class stratification, with its concomitant feelings of envy and inferiority, and its barriers to uninhibited mingling between the classes.

This is rightly seen as the quintessence of Croslandism. It is not without its difficulties, though. Most of them live within those two words 'egalitarian enough', and especially 'enough'. It is clear that a belief in some kind of equality (or equal worth) is integral to socialism. But it is also clear that the concept has proved a source of perennial difficulty. If it has taxed philosophers, it is not surprising that its political life has been fraught with problems. Its adherents seem to have spent most of their time trying to explain what it does not mean. Hence the attempt to set up intellectual base camps around notions of removing justifiable inequalities, or the political preference for an easier rhetoric of social justice. This suggests that it may be more sensible to approach the question of 'enough' from a different direction.

The current interest in issues of social inclusion (and exclusion) points the way forward. For, at bottom, socialism is an argument about citizenship. It asserts as a matter of belief (in equal worth) that access to the attributes of civilised life – political, social, economic, cultural – should be available to all, as far as this is practically possible. It is a doctrine of social inclusion. What has offended the traditional exponents of egalitarian socialism – such as Orwell,

Tawney, and Crosland – is the chasm that class division opens up. Tawney's great essay on equality was really an argument for what he called a common culture. His answer to the question about how much equality was necessary was that it should be enough to make a community. When the Webbs promulgated their National Minimum of Civilised Life, it was an argument about inclusion. There will always be room for disagreement about how much is enough. More useful, though, than the old familiar juggling with the relationship between opportunity, condition and outcome is to be clear that the aim is to give everyone a proper share in the means of civilised life. This is not revisionism. It is what socialism has really always been about. At a time when a new underclass is excluded and disconnected from the life available to others – without jobs, on sink estates, with grotty schools, in poor health – an inclusive politics of reconnection urgently defines any kind of new socialism.

This takes us from ideas to applications. It also takes us from the intellectual bravura of the early Crosland to the political agonies of the later. If he reinvented social democracy in the 1950s, he watched its disintegration in the 1970s. His prospectus for pain-free redistribution and generous public spending on the back of high and sustained economic growth had become the reality of an economy in inflationary crisis and of a state overwhelmed by demands it could not meet. Fiscal socialism had been replaced by the fiscal crisis of the state. It was a bad time to be a Croslandite social democrat, especially if you were Tony Crosland. The years that followed were even worse. Social democratic revisionism had replaced a socialism of public ownership with a socialism of taxing, spending, and redistributing. Now it found itself in need of revision. But of what kind?

The honest answer is that we are not quite sure, at least not yet. We are exploring uncharted political territory, in a world without maps. Both old social democracy and new neoliberal conservatism, each brimming with historical confidence at different moments in the recent past, are a busted flush. New Labour is still a practice without a theory, making it up as it goes along. This is why its friends have difficulty in describing it and why its critics have difficulty in framing a consistent line of attack. None of this need be unsettling, except for those fearful of fresh thinking. It is an exciting time for social and political theorists. It is also a good time for the social democratic left. After years of intellectual demoralisation, there is a new confidence emerging. Political recovery is matched, at last, with intellectual recovery. An old social democracy might have died, but a new social democracy shows signs of being born.

Its shape is still fuzzy and it lacks a label. The language of 'third way' and 'radical centre' begins to map a direction, though. At its centre is the task of combining a dynamic market economy with social cohesion and social justice, and the terms on which such a combination can be effected. It means a dense relationship between state and market very different from the old 'mixed economy' of separate ownership spheres. It requires an active state committed to the politics of social inclusion, attacking the blockages to citizenship in a sustained and coordinated way. It links an adherence to the conditions for macroeconomic stability with supply-side interventionism. It reconfigures the political system and explores new institutional models. It confounds the old demarcation lines of leftness and rightness in search of a new synthesis.

Where does all this leave Crosland? Still with plenty to say. Social inclusion means public spending; and this means a priority for public spending over tax cuts in the fiscal distribution of the dividends of growth. It also means a distribution of resources and opportunities towards those who need them most. Taxes remain a condition of citizenship; and if they are not to be found in one way they will have to be found in other ways. But Crosland(ism) takes us only so far. Socialism is not defined by the size of the state's welfare bill any more than it is defined by the extent of public ownership. It can represent failure, not success. Measuring public services by the amount of money that goes into them rather than by the effectiveness of what comes out of them (of which schools are the leading example, with Crosland as a prime culprit) has been a major error. In some respects, then, we have to fashion a post-Croslandite social democracy. Yet in doing so we should remember that his most remarkable achievement of all was to introduce us to a future – unstuffy, classless, fair, fun – in which people might actually want to live. This is not a bad model for us.

Note

1. At this period the Joseph Rowntree Foundation paid for a small number of appointments of research assistants to senior members of the shadow Cabinet. They were popularly known as 'chocolate soldiers'.

16 Postscript*
Susan Crosland

For nine of the 13 years we were married, Tony was a senior cabinet minister. On weekdays, his knowledge of his stepdaughters' crises had often to be second-hand. Sometimes Sheila and Ellen-Craig resented having to wait until the weekend to put their thoughts to him.

I had acquired the British custom of cooking a joint for Sunday lunch. When the throes of my daughters' adolescence were upon us, I jettisoned that custom, the mood at table being too unpredictable to warrant much culinary effort. Tony's opening question – 'What have you been up to this week?' – might well receive the answer 'Nothing", intending to irritate, always succeeding. In Opposition they could get to him – at him – more easily, to please, provoke, or seek understanding when none came from me.

He never sought to ingratiate himself with his stepdaughters: from early childhood they had to defend their views. He could be uncomfortably brusque if Sheila made a sweeping statement in favour, say, of censorship because she'd been so distressed by *Clockwork Orange* that she had to leave the cinema halfway through:

> You're perfectly capable of reading reviews, Sheila. That film has been described in every national newspaper. No one forced you to go to it. I haven't the faintest desire to see *Clockwork Orange*. That doesn't mean others shouldn't see it if that's how they want to spend their time.

On some subjects, having brooded, the children discovered an answer to his case. Sheila would then raise

---
* Written for this volume.

the matter for a second confrontation, so to speak. Ellen-Craig, being younger, had not yet developed the technique: 'The trouble is, Mama, I can never think of the answer when Tony's there. It's only afterwards, and then it's too late.'

> It's not too late. He'll be impressed. Go knock on the study door, say you know he's working now but could you make an appointment to see him later for twenty minutes as you now have the answer to his argument. For heaven's sake, write it down and take your notes with you. Otherwise you may lose the thread. Also, when he sees you have a piece of paper with your points, he'll want you to win the argument.

The essays we have read do just that. They have in common a theme which was central to *The Future of Socialism* – the difference between means and ends. All 15 writers have set out their points with candour and force. A number of their policies – the means – are sharply at odds with those which Tony put forward 40 years ago. Policies are not writ in stone. They are the means to the end. Where his arguments have proved wrong, they must be changed. What matters is the principled ideal – the end.

In *The Future of Socialism* he acknowledged this himself.

> A limit exists to the degree of equality which is desirable... But where en route, before we reach some drab extreme, we shall wish to stop, I have no idea. Our society will look quite different when we have carried through the changes mentioned earlier; and the whole argument will then need to be re-stated, and thought out afresh, by a younger generation than mine.

Index

Note: certain terms, to which reference is continually made, such as Equality, Labour Party, New Labour, Socialism and, of course, Crosland himself, have been excluded from the index.

Aerospace industry, 58
Anthony Crosland: the Mixed Economy, 3
Attlee, C. 51

Beaverbrook Press, 51, 54
Benefits, 33, 45–6
Benn, Tony, 57
Bernstein, Eduard, 3, 14
Bevan, Aneurin, 49
Binary system, 53, 62–3
Blair, Tony, 7, 9, 16
Board of Trade, President of, 62
Boyle, Sir Edward, 61
Britain's Economic Problem, 3
Brivati, Brian, ix
Brown, George, 58
Brown, Gordon, ix, 8, 35–48
Burnham, James, 22

Callaghan, James, 2, 7, 58, 64, 66
Capital, 38
Capitalism, 21, 23, 26, 32, 51
Child benefit, 47
Chipped White Cups of Dover, The, 50
Churchill, Winston, 49
Circular 10/65, 61–2
Class, social, 14–15, 22
Classless society, 36, 44
Clause Four, 16
Cole, G.D.H., 4
Cole, Humphrey, ix, 8
Collective provision, 1
Command economy, 39
Common ownership, 21

Comprehensive schools, 6, 16, 27, 53, 60–2
Computers, 38
Conrad, Joseph, 15
Conservative Enemy, The, 3, 43, 44
Constitutional reform, 13
Consumers' Party, 50
Controls, 37
Co-operative movement, 57
Council of Europe, 65
Cripps, Sir Stafford, 58
Critique of the Gotha Programme, The, 20
Crosland, Susan, ix, 8, 35, 53
Crosland's Future: Opportunity and Outcome, 3
Crossman, Richard, 59

Dalton, Hugh, 3–4
Democratic equality, 24, 26, 27, 28, 37, 43, 44, 45
Descartes, René, 64
Devaluation, 58
Disabled, the, 33, 45
Docker, Lady, 51, 54
Dodd, Philip, ix–x
Durbin, Evan, 4

Economic Affairs, Department of, 58
Economic growth, 6–7, 26, 27, 39, 51, 52
Economic liberalism, 28–32
Economist, The, vii, 7
Education Secretary, 5–6, 61
Education, 16, 25, 26, 27, 30, 38, 39, 40, 41

205

Index

Educational opportunity, 43
11-plus selection, 61
Eliot, T.S., 26
Employment opportunity, 43
Environment, Department of, 63
Equality of opportunity, 24–5, 26, 29, 33–4, 37, 40–4
Equality of outcome, 24, 26, 31, 37, 42
European Community, 64–5

Fabian Society, vii, 3, 7
Family backgrounds, 25–7
Foot, Michael, 15, 17
Foreign Office, 2
Foreign Secretary, 57, 59, 64–6
Foster, Sir Christopher, vii
France, 45
Full employment, 38, 51
Future, 51, 52, 57, 61
Future of Socialism, The, 1, 3, 5, 6, 14, 25, 35, 36, 40

Gaitskell, Hugh, 1, 2, 3, 49, 57, 59
General Theory of Employment, Interest and Money, 23
Genetic endowment, 25–7, 40
Germany, 5, 45
Globalisation, 14, 32, 37–8, 44
Gordon Walker, Patrick, 60
Greenwood, Anthony, 57
Grimsby, 65

Hattersley, Frederick, 60–1
Hattersley, Roy, x, 8, 57–66
Healey, Denis, 2
Heath, Edward, 58
Higher education, 6, 42, 53, 62–3
Horney, Karen, 51, 54
Housing, 44
Housing and Local Government, Minister of, 63

Icelandic fishing dispute, 65

IMF crisis, 64, 65–6
Individual Learning Accounts, 46
Industrial democracy, 43–4
Inheritance tax, 31
Inherited wealth, 44
Intelligence tests, 40

Jay, Douglas, 4
Jenkins, Roy, 2, 60
Jones, Inigo, 59

Katwala, Sunder, vii
Kellner, Peter, x
Keynes, J.M., 13, 22, 23, 51
Kissinger, Henry, 59

Labour government (1997–), 28–34
Labour market, 31–2, 34, 38, 45
Leonard, Dick, x, 1–9
Leonard, Mark, vii
Levelling-up, 27
Leyton by-election, 60
Life-long education 48
Life-long learning, 30
Lipsey, David, x–xi, 8, 13–17
Long-term sick, 45
LSE library, 3

Macmillan, Harold, 61
Management, 21–2
Managerial revolution, 21
Markets, 23–4, 29, 31, 32
Marshall, Alfred, 3
Marx, Karl, 20–4
Means and ends, 9, 15, 36
Means of production, 20–3, 51
Meritocracy, 25–6
Mikardo, Ian, 57–8
Minimum wage, 44, 45
Mixed economy, 20, 24, 39
Mulley, Fred, 57

National Assistance, 33
National Health Service, 16
National minimum wage, 31

Index

Nationalisation (*see also* Public ownership), 21, 24, 36, 58
New Right, 27–8
New Right, 40
1963 Club, 59

Open University, 63
Operation Neptune, 59
Ownership, 21
Oxford Union, 1, 58

Palliser, Sir Michael, xi, 8
Pigou, A.C., 3
Plant, Raymond, xi, 8, 19–34, 40
Pluralism, 24
Plymouth Brethren, 52
Polytechnics, 62–3
Poverty, 29, 31, 34, 38, 45, 47
Price, Christopher, xi, 6, 8
Private life, 53
Private ownership, 51
Property-owning democracy, 44
Proportional representation, 13
Prospect, vii
Public expenditure, 29, 39, 65
Public ownership, 15–16, 39
Public schools, 5–6, 52–3
Public Schools' Commission, 6, 53
Public Sector Borrowing Requirement, 66
Public services, 15–16

Rawls, John, 24–5
Redistributive taxation, 5, 65
Reisman, David, xi–xii, 3–6
Rent of ability, 26, 28, 42
Revisionism, 13–17, 28, 32
Richards, Paul, vii
Rise of the Meritocracy, The, 50
Robbins, Lord, 63

School-leaving age, 62
Shareholding, 21
Single parents, 45–7
Smethwick, 60

Social Democratic Party, 13
Social exclusion, 30–1, 33, 34
Social justice, 19, 20, 21, 24, 27, 33, 39, 40
Socialism Now, 3, 24, 25, 26, 40
Soviet Union, 5
Stewart, Michael, 60
Sweden, 4–6

Tawney, R.H., 4, 9, 42
Tax cutting, 7, 15
Tax payers, 33
Tax and spend policies, 6–7, 39
Taxes, 27, 45–6
Thatcher, Margaret, 32, 62
Thatcher, Margaret, 62
Theory of Justice, A, 25
Trade unions, 23
Treasury, 2, 37, 49, 63, 64
Trickle-down effect, 28
Typhoon, 15

Unemployment, 7, 15, 30, 33, 37, 45, 47, 48
United States, 4–6, 45
Universities, 62–3
University for Industry, 46

Vaizey, John, 6
Values, 19–20, 36

Welfare reform, 34
Welfare state, 23, 39, 45, 46
Welfare-to-work, 17, 33
Williams, Philip, 3
Williams, Shirley, 52, 62
Wilson, Harold, 2, 58, 59, 60, 63, 64
Wincott, Daniel, xii
Women, 35, 46–7
Working Families' Tax Credit, 47
Wright, Tony, xii, 8, 193–201

Young, Michael, xii, 4, 6, 8, 49ff, 63